DISCOVERY AND EXPLORATION

THE GREAT AGE OF EXPLORATION

BY DUNCAN CASTLEREAGH

International Learning Systems
Corporation Limited · London

Executive coordinators: Beppie Harrison
John Mason
Design director: Guenther Radtke
Editorial: Ann Craig
Jill Gormley
Marjorie Dickens
Picture Editor: Peter Cook
Research: Margery MacLaren
Cartography by Geographical Projects

This edition specially produced in 1973
for International Learning Systems
Corporation Limited, London
by Aldus Books Limited, London.

Printed and bound in Yugoslavia by
Mladinska Knjiga, Ljubljana

THE GREAT AGE OF EXPLORATION

Contents

Left: Portuguese ships like the one in which Magellan sailed to India in 1505 in the fleet of Francisco de Almeida

Frontispiece: a battle on land and sea between the Portuguese and Arabs at Surat, just north of Bombay, India

List of Maps

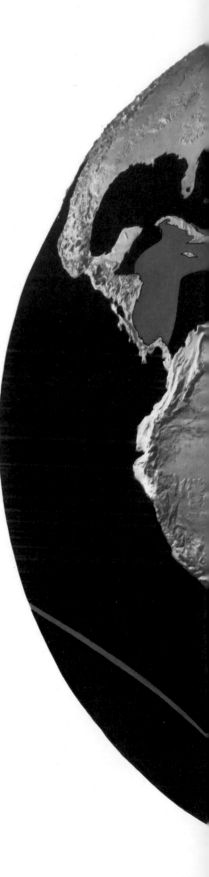

The illuminated globe shows the areas that gradually became known as the men of the Great Age of Exploration pushed open the horizons of their Mediterranean world, south as they tried to reach India, west as they crossed the vast ocean to seek China.

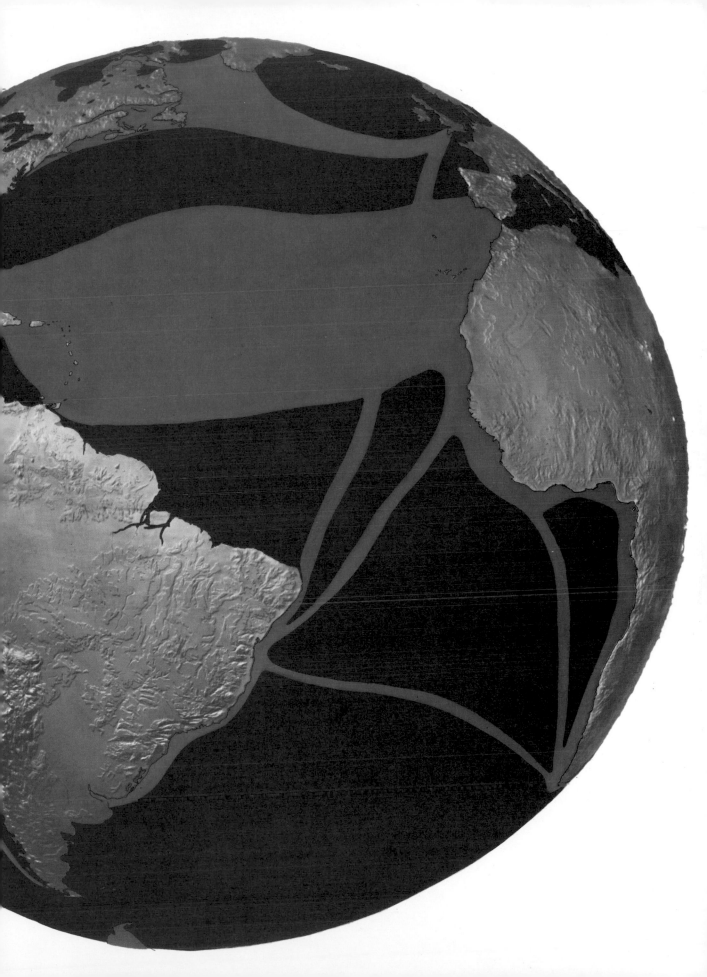

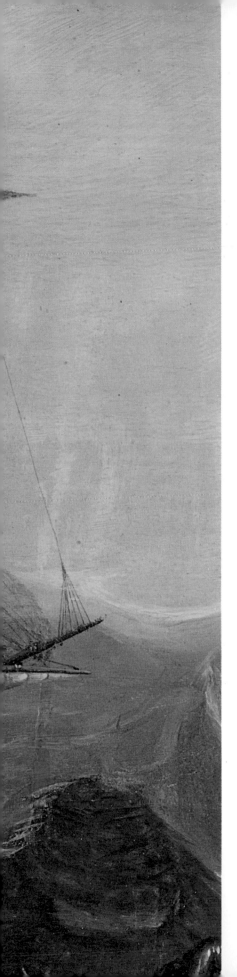

The Historical Challenge
1

One day, late in the summer of 1522, a small and sorry-looking vessel limped into the harbor of Sanlucar de Barrameda in southern Spain. Her foretopmast, damaged in a storm, creaked painfully under the pressure of the light wind in her sails. Her timbers were worm-eaten and heavy with barnacles. Her seams were leaking so badly that for weeks past only round-the-clock pumping had kept her afloat.

The 17 men aboard the tiny vessel presented a heart-rending sight. Of the ship's original complement of 50 officers and sailors, they alone had survived the rigors of their voyage, and even they were half-dead from starvation, scurvy, and sheer exhaustion.

Yet to all who saw them, the battered *Victoria* and the ragged men aboard her appeared wreathed in glory. They had made history's first voyage round the world.

The *Victoria's* achievement was a remarkable one by any standards. But perhaps the most significant thing about it was that it occurred less than a century after European sailors had first begun venturing beyond the confines of their own coastal waters. Before 1422, none but the Vikings had ever sailed more than 800 miles into the vast oceans beyond Europe's shores. Yet by 1522, when the *Victoria* made her famous voyage, Christopher Columbus had already discovered the New World and Portuguese mariners were making regular trips to the Far East.

What had happened in the short span of 100 years to transform Europe's coast-hugging seamen into world-ranging explorers? What combination of factors had conspired to launch the brilliant period of exploration we now call "the great age of discovery"?

The best way to answer these questions is, perhaps, to consider the historical forces which, in preceding centuries, had made far-flung exploration not only unthinkable but impossible. It is necessary, therefore, to go back in history as far as the 400's, when the western half of the great Roman Empire fell to barbarian invaders from the north and east.

When Rome fell, her conquerors carved out for themselves numerous small kingdoms in the provinces she had once ruled. But rivalry for more land and power led to constant conflict among them. And,

Left: it was in ships such as this that the early navigators sailed from Portugal on their voyages of exploration and conquest. Buffeted by storms and hampered by contrary winds, these sturdy vessels enabled the gallant seamen to penetrate unknown regions. The Portuguese established colonies and trading stations and tried to spread Christianity throughout Africa.

after two centuries of warfare and upheaval, little of the old Roman culture remained in western Europe except Christianity, the religion adopted by the Roman Empire in her last days of power.

During this period of turmoil, the system of mutual protection and support that we call feudalism developed. Rulers of small kingdoms granted land and privileges to lesser lords in exchange for their allegiance and military support. In turn, these lesser lords gave peasants the right to live under their protection in exchange for working their land.

World map, based on Gall's projection, showing the main geographical features.

Because continual warfare made travel unsafe, and because each feudal estate produced all that its inhabitants needed, trade—and with it, towns—declined during the early Middle Ages. And, as trade and city life ground to a halt, so too did the exchange of ideas upon which the advancement of learning depended. The one great civilizing force in Europe at this time was the Church, whose doctrines dominated medieval thought, and in whose monasteries such classical learning as still existed was kept alive.

It was to be several centuries before trade, towns, and learning

reawakened in western Europe, and even longer before powerful nation-states emerged.

In the meantime, one important sector of the Roman Empire had not succumbed to the barbarian invaders. This was the eastern half of the empire, which included Asia Minor, Greece and its islands, and the lands now occupied by Lebanon, Syria, Israel, and Egypt. While the last vestiges of the old Roman order were disappearing in the West, this eastern region—which came to be called the Byzantine Empire—was flourishing. In fact, its capital, Byzantium (later called Constantinople, and later still Istanbul), was experiencing a golden age of power, prosperity, culture, and learning.

Not surprisingly, the Byzantine Empire's wealth and power made it the frequent target of would-be conquerors. From the north and west it was assailed by the barbarians; from the east by the Persians; and from the south by a new and dangerous enemy, the Arabs.

The Arabs of northern Africa were Moslems, followers of the new religion called Islam, founded by the prophet Mohammed in the early 600's. They embarked on a determined effort to spread their religion by conquest. Between the late 600's and the early 800's, they succeeded in wresting from Byzantium the territories that now make up Syria,

Left: Rumeli Hissar Fort, Istanbul, Turkey, is typical of the fortifications built around Constantinople (later Istanbul). The city was founded by Constantine the Great in A. D. 328 from the ancient city of Byzantium. Walls were built around the city, giving complete protection on all sides. The western wall was damaged by earthquake in 447 and was replaced by three walls 20 yards apart, each flanked by 96 towers. These formed a barricade about 200 feet thick and 100 feet high, in which were housed troops and equipment to meet any foe. These walls, which were restored from time to time, defied barbarous assaults for more than a thousand years.

Lebanon, Israel, and Egypt. And, by the middle of the 900's the Moslem Empire stretched unbroken from western India to the Atlantic shores of northern Africa. During this great period of conquest, Moslem Moors—a people originating in northwestern Africa—even reached Europe. They established themselves in the Iberian Peninsula, site of present-day Spain and Portugal.

For a time, it seemed that the Byzantine Empire would succumb to the Moslems. Ultimately, however, the Byzantines staged a comeback, and managed to drive the Moslems back on several fronts. In fact, by about A.D. 1000, the Byzantine Empire was once more strong enough to begin expanding again. But just at this point, an aggressive and powerful new enemy, the Moslem Turks, invaded from the east. Within a short space of time, the Turks had made such inroads into Byzantine defenses that the security of the entire empire was threatened.

A number of powerful kingdoms—among them England, France, and the Holy Roman Empire—had, by this time, begun to emerge in western Europe. And, on the Mediterranean coast, the republics of Venice and Genoa were already showing signs of becoming great sea powers. It was to Christendom, then, that the beleaguered Byzantine Empire turned for help against the Moslem Turks in the 1000's. (Ironically, the empire was ultimately to suffer as much, if not more, at the

Above: Islam, the Moslem religion, was founded by Mohammed in the late 500's or early 600's. It is based on the word of the Koran (through which God is said to have revealed himself to Mohammed) and the sayings and way of life of the prophet himself. Followers of the creed are required, among other things, to worship God five times a day, with the worshiper facing Mecca. Early Moslem conquests spread the Islamic doctrine far and wide and by the mid-900's the empire reached from North Africa to eastern India. This picture shows Mohammed taking part in a siege.

hands of its Christian allies than in the struggles against the Moslems.)

The men of western Christendom were only too glad to take up the cudgels against the Moslems. Sporadic fighting between Christians and Moslems in the Iberian Peninsula and in the islands of the Mediterranean had been going on since the 800's. But the time had now come for a concerted Christian effort against the infidels.

Thus began the series of "Holy Wars" known as the Crusades, which continued for almost two centuries (1096–1270). But however much they tried, the crusaders never succeeded in gaining more than a few temporary advantages over the Moslems. Indeed, the Crusades merely served to prove beyond a doubt that Christendom had neither the unity nor the strength of arms to push the Moslems back from the eastern and southern shores of the Mediterranean.

The Crusades produced a further source of frustration in revealing to the men of Christendom what riches lay beyond their reach. At the eastern end of the Mediterranean, they had seen the profusion of rich commodities which poured into the Moslem Empire from the Orient: silks, spices, tapestries, porcelain, and precious stones. Once seen, such goods were earnestly desired. Unfortunately, they could be had only on terms dictated by the Moslems, whose strategic geographical position gave them control over all East-West trade. In fact, the Mos-

Right: reproduction of an illumination from an Arabic manuscript of 1200, showing the Saracen army on the march against the crusaders. The campaigns undertaken by Christians from western Europe between 1096 and 1270, "the Crusades," endeavored to prevent the spread of Islam and to regain territories won by the Moslems. The attempt failed to weaken the Moslem empire, but the crusaders established a "Latin Empire" in Byzantium which allowed the flow of ancient works back to the west.

Above: Peter the Hermit, priest of Amiens, whose oratory attracted many pilgrims to the first crusade. Their journey to Constantinople was one of the preliminary acts of the first crusade. Peter reached Constantinople in July, 1096, but the crusaders were routed by the Turks (whom they attacked against Peter's wishes), leaving him to await the princes in May, 1097. Photo by Denise Bourbonnais, from Bibliotheque de l'Arsenal, Paris.

Above: view of Venice from a manuscript of 1338 showing St. Marks and the Doge's Palace. The former was originally the private chapel of the Doge, richly decorated with materials from the East. The latter is the head of state's official residence. After the crusades, Venice was a thriving center of trade, her merchants buying from the Moors coveted goods from the Orient, for resale elsewhere in Europe at higher prices. MS. Bodley 264. Fol. 218.

lem barrier to Western commerce with the East was so formidable that it had been penetrated only by a few rare travelers such as Marco Polo in the second half of the 1200's.

The Moslems had firmly established themselves at the crossroads between East and West when Christendom was weak and disorganized. Now, when towns and commerce were beginning to flourish once more in western Europe, Christendom found itself cut off from the richest sources of world trade. Only the city-states of Venice and Genoa profited from this situation, for they possessed a trade monopoly with

the Moslems. Eastern goods reached the shores of the Mediterranean via caravan routes, the Indian Ocean, the Red Sea, and Egypt. Once in Mediterranean ports, they were sold by Moslem traders to Venetian and Genoese merchants, who then proceeded to sell them elsewhere in Europe at exorbitant prices.

After Christendom's repeated efforts to weaken the Moslem Empire had failed, the trade barrier stood firmer than ever. The remaining possibility was to seek an alternative route to the East—an ocean route that would completely bypass the Mediterranean and its Moslem-held shores. But the search for such a route would entail voyaging far out into unknown Atlantic waters, and it was to be almost two centuries before any European mariners would attempt a feat so daring.

In the meantime, Europe had to content itself with obtaining the Eastern luxuries it wanted from Venice and Genoa. In any case, most of the western kingdoms had, by the 1300's, grown weary of fighting the Moslems, and were preoccupied with other matters. The Holy

Right: the Palacio de Generalife (Palace of the Architect) in Granada, one of the outlying buildings con- nected with the Alhambra, the ancient palace and fortress originally built by the Moorish Kings between 1284 and 1354. Considered to be one of the finest examples of Moorish art in Europe, it has been restored many times. Granada, a maritime province of southern Spain, became the leading city of Moorish Spain when Córdoba fell to Ferdinand of Castile in 1236.

Above: quayside of the Portuguese capital of Lisbon. Portugal was dominated by the Moors from A.D. 711, but in 1147, Alfonso I incorporated Lisbon into his kingdom. For centuries the city suffered earthquakes and in 1755 was reduced to ruin by a simultaneous devastating earthquake and tidal wave.

Roman Empire was pursuing a policy of expansion; France and England were at war with each other; and the Italian city-states were experiencing the dawn of the Renaissance.

Only in the Iberian Peninsula was the crusading spirit still very much alive. There the struggle to oust the Moslem Moors had continued for centuries. And by the late 1200's this unceasing effort had succeeded in driving the Moors out of every part of the peninsula except the south, where the Moslem kingdom of Granada still remained strong.

The three Christian kingdoms in Iberia were Aragon, Castile, and Portugal. All three were coastal seafaring nations. All three were determined enemies of the Moslems. As it was becoming clear that the Moslems would never release their hold on East-West trade, all three might have been expected to seek an alternative sea route to the East. But Aragon's sole coast was on the Mediterranean, and it was content to confine its maritime interests to that sea. Castile, possessing both an Atlantic and a Mediterranean coastline, was kept busy defending its southern border with Granada.

Of the three Iberian kingdoms, Portugal alone possessed both the political and the geographical advantages necessary for the development of interest in ocean exploration. Portugal's only land frontier was with Castile. More important still, its only coastline was along the Atlantic.

Right: political map of Europe, with the governments of approximately 1400.

19

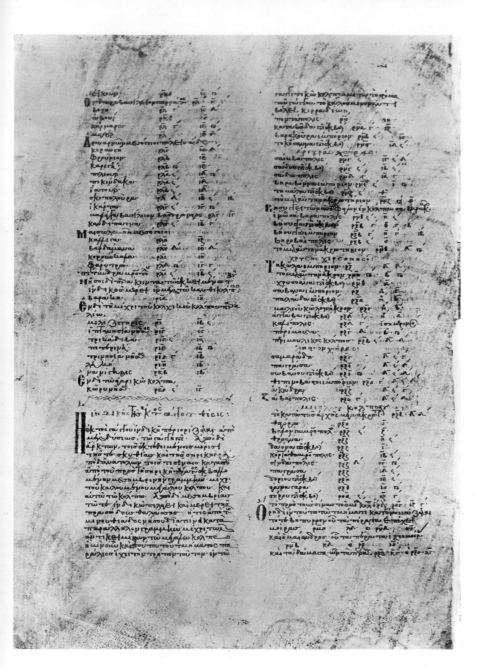

Left: from Vatican Codex Urbinas Graecus 82, an early Greek manuscript of Ptolemy's *Geography*, in which he attempted to build up a dependable map of the world then inhabited, from the study of the latitude and longitude of the main points on its surface. This page shows his system for the location and siting of places in India.

Because the Atlantic offered Portugal its only highway to the outside world, it was, from the beginning, a nation of seafarers. Soon after the little kingdom emerged from Moorish domination in 1143, Portugal founded its own fighting navy. According to legend this infant navy succeeded in capturing an entire Moorish fleet off Lisbon, Portugal's capital, as early as 1150. By 1300, the Portuguese navy had its own admiral and a score of Genoese pilots to captain its ships and train its crews. Meanwhile, growing numbers of Portuguese merchant vessels were plying the sea routes to France, England, and Flanders with goods for trade.

The largest of the Portuguese trading ships, the *naves,* were stout-decked sailing ships of 200 tons and more. And Portuguese seamen

were not content to confine their maritime activities to the familiar waters of their own and neighboring coasts. As early as 1341 they made the first recorded Portuguese visit to the Canary Islands, 800 miles southwest of the Iberian Peninsula.

But fear of the unknown kept the Portuguese from venturing farther into the Atlantic. They not only had no idea of what lay beyond the Canaries, but were unfamiliar with astronomy and mathematics, the two chief handmaidens of navigation. Like men everywhere in Europe at that time, the Portuguese knew less about these subjects—and about geography—than the ancient Greeks had known.

As far back as the 300's B.C., Greek philosophers had believed that the earth is round. By the 200's B.C., the principles of geometry had been worked out by Euclid, and the astronomer Eratosthenes had made a remarkably accurate estimate of the earth's circumference. And, in the A.D. 100's, a Greek mathematician, astronomer, and geographer named Ptolemy had written two great works summarizing all that was then known about astronomy and geography.

The Roman Empire had preserved this heritage of Greek learning. But, in the upheaval that followed the fall of the empire, most of it had been lost. In the monasteries of western Europe, some classical writings had survived, but they were by and large purely philosophical, rather than scientific works.

The ancients' contributions to mathematics, astronomy, and geography did, however, eventually find their way back to Europe—by an extremely roundabout route. One place where the learning of the classical scientists had been preserved was the Byzantine Empire. And one of the Moslems' first conquests was the Byzantine territory of Syria. Here the conquerors came into contact with the writings of the ancient Greeks. They translated these important works into Arabic for their own use, and later took copies of them to the great universities which they established in the Iberian Peninsula.

For many years, the Moslem universities in Iberia were open only to Moslems and to Jews (who had begun settling in the Iberian Peninsula long before the Moslem conquest). But as the Christian reconquest of Iberia proceeded, the Moslem universities fell one by one into Christian hands. Not all the Moslem and Jewish scholars who taught in them were banished. Many stayed on, some after undergoing a real or nominal conversion to Christianity. They continued to work, translating the classical scientific works from Arabic into Latin, the lan-

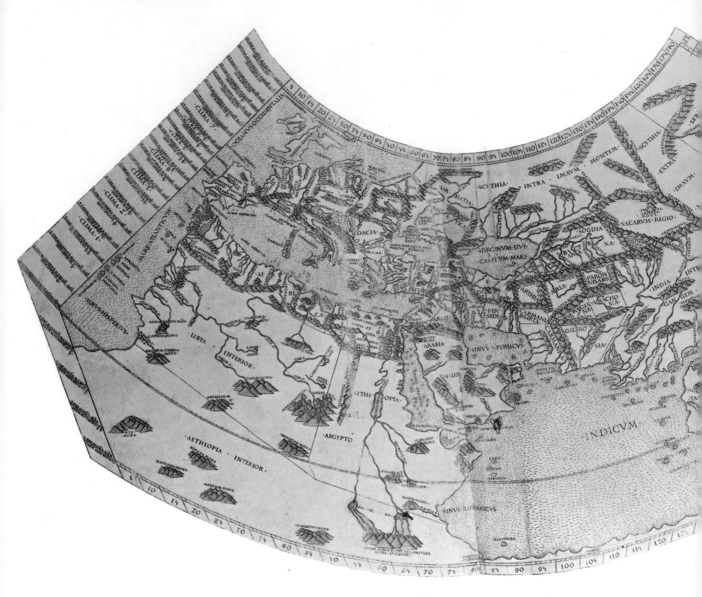

Above: world map from Ptolemy's *Geography*, Rome Edition of 1508. In this work Ptolemy tried to make geography a scientific study and a convenient and easy form of reference. As an astronomer he was able to explain the mathematical relationship of the earth and the celestial bodies. He divided the equatorial circle into parallels of latitude and meridians of longitude and within the framework thus created he outlined the then-known regions of the world.

guage which was then used by all educated European Christians.

Not long after this source of ancient learning had been opened to European scholars, another source also began to provide long-lost classical works. During the Holy Wars against the Moslems, the crusaders had established a so-called "Latin Empire" in Byzantium. From that center of culture and learning, at this time called Constantinople, ancient works now began flowing directly back to Christendom. The high-water mark of this flow was achieved in 1407, when a copy of Ptolemy's *Geography* reached the West. Within two years, Latin translations of it were available to European scholars.

As yet, however, the great works of classical learning had been seen only by scholars. Printing was still to be invented, and the useful manuscripts becoming available were rare and costly. Furthermore, only educated men well versed in Latin could read them. So, despite the recovery of Ptolemy's *Geography* and other scientific works of the past, most people remained in ignorance of astronomy, mathematics,

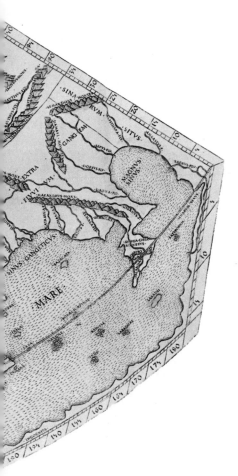

Right: Henry the Navigator (1394—1460). With his two elder brothers he took part in the conquest of Ceuta, during which he realized the importance of seapower against the Moslem enemies. Third son of King John I of Portugal, Prince Henry spent a great part of his life encouraging Portuguese exploration, spending most of his personal fortune in the process. He founded a school of navigation and mapmaking, where he employed experts not only to train captains and pilots, but also to interpret the information they brought back from their voyages. His encouragement led, after his death, to the circumnavigation of Africa and the discovery of an ocean route to the Orient from Europe.

and geography. It was, for example, still widely believed that the earth was flat.

Ocean exploration could not possibly be undertaken by mariners ignorant of the basic principles of navigation. What was needed was a man who could bridge the gap between the scholars and the sailors, a man who possessed both learning and a vital interest in pushing back the frontiers of navigation. He would have to be a man of daring and determination, for any plan to explore the unknown would be met with strong opposition by mariners and landsmen alike. He would also have to be a man of great persuasion, for any serious attempt to explore the unknown would take masterly organization and tremendous financial backing.

Fortunately for the history of exploration, just such a man came forward at this time. And perhaps it is no coincidence that he was born a prince of Portugal, the little nation of seafarers whose only highway to the world was the broad Atlantic.

Response
2

In August, 1385, Castile suddenly launched a full-scale invasion against Portugal. The Portuguese Army was heavily outnumbered, but aided by a small force of English troops, they won a resounding victory. The resultant strengthening of existing Portuguese-English ties led to the marriage of King John (João) of Portugal to Philippa, the daughter of John of Gaunt. The royal match was to have historic consequences—not only for Portugal, but for the whole of Europe—for it produced the remarkable prince who was to set in motion the great age of discovery: Henry the Navigator.

Prince Henry was the third son born to the royal couple, and so third in order of succession to the throne. Ordinarily, such a position in the royal hierarchy would have left the prince with a lifetime of court and ministerial duties. Circumstances decreed otherwise. When Henry was 21 a dramatic event changed the whole course of his life.

As a boy, Henry and his elder brothers, Edward (Duarte) and Peter (Pedro), received their religious training and general education from their devout and learned mother. And their father, the king, instructed them in the arts of war and the code of chivalry.

By the time the princes had reached their late teens, all three were eager to win knighthood, proof of a young man's personal honor and courage. Traditionally, however, knighthood could be won only in battle, and Portugal was now at peace with Castile. Nevertheless, King John sympathized with his sons' ambition, and offered them an alternative path to the title they coveted. He would hold a year-long series of jousts and tourneys, during which they would have ample opportunity to distinguish themselves.

But the king's plan did not satisfy the young princes. They wanted to make their reputations in battle as their father had done. One day, while they were wishing aloud for a real war in which to prove themselves, they were overheard by the king's treasurer. This thrifty gentleman might have shuddered at the thought of having to raise money for a war to gratify the romantic ambitions of three royal youths. How-

Left: in 1387, the marriage between King John I of Portugal and Philippa, eldest daughter of England's John of Gaunt, helped to strengthen the ties between the two countries. This royal union is best remembered for one of its remarkable offspring, Prince Henry, the Navigator.

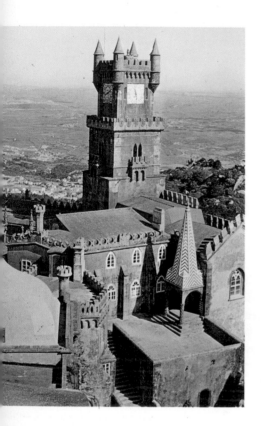

Above: the Portuguese royal family maintained a fortress at Pena Palace, Sintra, from the 1100's to the 1300's. Later the fortress was rebuilt, partly in deliberate imitation of a medieval fortress and partly using a monastery that had replaced the original fortress.

ever, at that particular time, he happened to have been turning over in his mind a certain military expedition. This project, he calculated, would not only satisfy the yearnings of the three princes, but also, if successful, bring great financial advantages to Portugal. What he could not know, however, was that it would set Henry on his momentous path of exploration and discovery.

The treasurer had been told by a servant (who had once been a Moslem prisoner) about the wealth of the northern African port of Ceuta. According to the servant, the city was wide open to attack from the sea.

While mulling over the benefits to Portugal of a successful attack against Ceuta, the treasurer had also been considering the cost of a year of lavish feasts and tourneys. Surely an expedition against the port of Ceuta was a more profitable way of spending the king's money. So the royal money-keeper commended the young men for their noble ambitions, and suggested that they try to persuade their father to make war on Ceuta.

At first, the king refused to take their proposal seriously. In the whole history of the struggle to retake the Iberian Peninsula from the Moslems, no serious blow had ever been leveled at Moslem-held northern Africa. In fact, it was from Ceuta itself that the Moslems launched many invasions against Christendom. So it was hard to believe that this Moslem stronghold could actually be as vulnerable as the treasurer reported it to be. King John pointed out to his sons the immense dangers and difficulties of the expedition they proposed, and urged them to think again. They were determined, however, and Prince Henry, the spokesman for the three brothers, gradually overcame his father's objections.

A main concern of King John was the possible military repercussions of the venture. If Portugal succeeded in taking Ceuta, he argued, then the Moslem kingdom of Granada, which depended heavily on help and supplies from that port, would fall prey to the military might of Castile. And with Granada out of the way, Castile would be certain to turn her forces against her old enemy, Portugal.

In dealing with this objection, Henry revealed the strong crusading spirit that was later to be a driving force behind his campaign of discovery. To take Moslem Ceuta, he argued, would be to render a service to God. By the same token, to withhold that service, for fear it might help Castile, would be a sin against God. "Even if the king of Castile were our greatest enemy," he concluded, "he would be so only by acci-

Above: the port of Ceuta at the southeastern end of the Strait of Gibraltar which the Portuguese captured from the Moors in the 1400's. Right: the Strait of Gibraltar is 31 miles long, and between the Rock of Gibraltar and Mount Atho, just east of Ceuta, the width is a mere 14 miles. These two forts controlled the passage between the known world of the Mediterranean and the almost unknown world of the Atlantic.

dent, for he is a Christian, as we are. The Moslems, on the other hand, are our enemies by nature." It was almost certainly this argument that persuaded the king to undertake the venture.

The first step was to scout out Ceuta's defenses without arousing suspicion. This was done by sending two galleys on a trumped-up diplomatic mission to Sicily. The two captains were instructed to drop anchor along the way (as if to rest their crews) as near as possible to Ceuta, and take careful note of all they saw.

One man, on his return from this scouting mission, built a model of Ceuta's defense works and sea approaches out of sand, ribbons, and beans. On this evidence, King John decided that a well-organized attack from the sea stood a very good chance of success, and began to prepare an expedition.

All three princes were given important responsibilities. To Henry fell the task of organizing the building and outfitting of ships and the assembling of crews in the northern part of the country, with Oporto serving as his headquarters. Peter had a similar task in the south, with

Above: Prince Henry the Navigator was driven by the urge to explore and extend his country's powers, but most strongly of all by his crusading spirit. His religious beliefs were deep and constant and he might well have worshiped in a church like this one, the Praia de Luz near Sagres.

headquarters in Lisbon. Edward, meanwhile, was put in charge of Portugal's financial affairs and given responsibility for the administration of justice in the kingdom. The king was thus left free to concentrate on the diplomatic problems that would inevitably arise, and to organize the supply of artillery and other armaments for the fleet.

For many months no one talked of anything but ships and munitions, particularly in Oporto and Lisbon. In these cities, there was hardly a soul not engaged in making ropes, fashioning casks, slaughtering cattle, and salting down beef, baking biscuits, catching and drying fish, caulking seams in hulls and decks, or packing bombards and cannons.

News of this build-up of arms and supplies could hardly be kept from the outside world. But, apart from the royal household, no one knew exactly where the great fleet was intended to strike. Both Castile and Granada took fright. But King John allayed their fears by sending an ultimatum to the Duke of Holland, and took care that everyone heard of it. At the same time, he notified the duke in secret that the ulti-

matum had been sent solely to deceive the real victims of the forthcoming attack. Even the Portuguese government was kept in the dark about the real target of the operation until the entire fleet was assembled near Lisbon and ready to sail. At that crucial point, Queen Philippa fell sick of the plague. She called her sons to her bedside and gave them each a sword and her blessing for the proposed expedition. She died a few days before the fleet sailed.

The citizens of Ceuta had no inkling of what was in store for them until the second week of August, 1414. Then they were confronted by more than 200 Portuguese vessels suddenly appearing off the coast of the tiny peninsula. The battle was short and decisive. The Portuguese landed at daybreak on August 15, and, after a single day of fierce hand-to-hand combat, the port fell.

During the fighting, the three princes proved their daring and bravery. As they had wished, they were tested—and found worthy—on the field of battle. With the swords given to them by their mother, they were now knighted by their father in the city they had helped to conquer.

Below: this illustration from the Nuremburg Chronicles shows boat-building in the 1400's, which was common to any seaport of the period. The typical Portuguese and Spanish ship was the caravel, the largest being the 50-ton ocean-going caravel for long voyages.

Left: an altarpiece by Nuno Gonçalves, painted about 1450, showing St. Vincent, patron saint of Lisbon, in the center. On his left, wearing a large hat, stands Henry the Navigator, with the future King John II, the boy in the conical hat. Kneeling in the foreground are Alfonso V, called "the African" because of his successes against the Moors in Africa, and his queen.

The conquest of Ceuta played a significant role in shaping Prince Henry's future, and with it, the future of the world. In helping to create the fighting fleet, he had come into contact with many experienced seamen and had learned that a well-provisioned ship could remain at sea for a long time. The capture of the port had also taught him how effective sea power could be against the Moslems. Moreover, while in Ceuta, he learned that the Moslem Empire extended far down the west coast of Africa—farther than any European had yet traveled. And he picked up valuable geographical information about Africa from the merchants of Ceuta who regularly plied the caravan routes that led south and west to the Guinea coast.

Back in Portugal, Prince Henry began to fit these and other bits of information together. How could they be used to further his most cherished ambition—to strike a crushing blow against the Moslem Empire?

Henry was Grand Master of the Order of Christ, a religious order sworn to fight the infidels. But he knew that, throughout most of Christendom, men had lost interest in waging crusades. He also knew the futility of mounting a Portuguese campaign against the Moslem Empire. For the little kingdom could not hope, on its own, to do more than it already had done against Moslems in the Mediterranean. But it now appeared that their empire stretched southward along Africa's west coast. If Portuguese ships could stay at sea long enough to explore the coast, Henry could learn just how strong Moslem defenses were in that quarter. If, as he strongly suspected, the Moslem Empire was weak at its farthest limits, it could be successfully attacked from the rear.

To undertake such a venture, Portugal would need allies. Here a medieval myth offered some hope. When the Moslem Empire had first begun to expand, a few pockets of Christianity had been trapped within its confines. Over the centuries a belief in the continued existence of such outposts of Christianity had combined with a little optimism to give rise to the legend of a powerful Christian kingdom. Ruled by one "Prester John," this kingdom was said to flourish somewhere deep inside Asia or Africa. This idea was universal in Europe from about the middle of the 1100's to the beginning of the 1300's. The Asiatic story then faded away but the name of the "priest king" remained and in the 1400's the legend was renewed, especially by Portuguese explorers. This time Prester John was specifically thought to be the

Above: Fez, capital of northern Morocco, where life for ordinary people has changed little over the centuries. Below: frontispiece from a book of 1540 showing Prester John, the legendary Christian priest-king of Moslem Asia.

Emperor of Ethiopia. Henry believed that if Portugal could make contact with Prester John, his aid could be enlisted against the Moslems. Although this contact never materialized, the belief at the time provided a further incentive to seek a way to the East.

To take up the "holy war" against Islam, from a new and as yet untried direction, was thus Prince Henry's chief motivation in beginning— as he was soon to do—his great campaign of exploration. However, he had further motives for wanting to explore the unknown. One was simply a craving to know more about the world. A chronicler of Portuguese history during this period, Gomes Eannes de Azurara, tells us that Prince Henry "wanted to know what lands were beyond the Canary Islands and Cape Bojador, for up to that time no one knew." Another strong incentive to exploration was a desire to increase Portugal's trading opportunities. According to Azurara, Henry believed "that if in these territories there should be any harbors where men could enter without peril, they could bring back much merchandise at little cost, because there would be no other persons to compete with them."

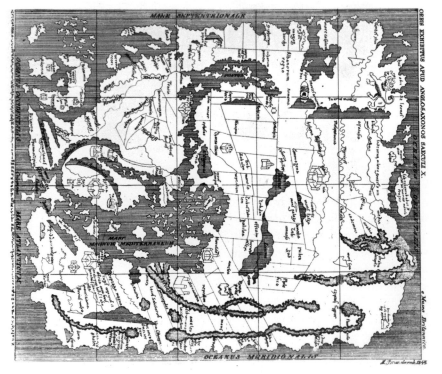

Left: the Latin inscription bordering this map attributes it to the 900's, but by modern reckoning it was probably drawn during the 1000's. It is possible that this map was seen by Henry the Navigator and encouraged his quest for a direct route to the east.

Right: this section of a Catalan map, using lines radiating from compass points as a form of grid, is attributed to Abraham de Gresques. Lavishly ornamented and on fine parchment, it was probably made for Charles V of France, but it could have been put to practical use.

34

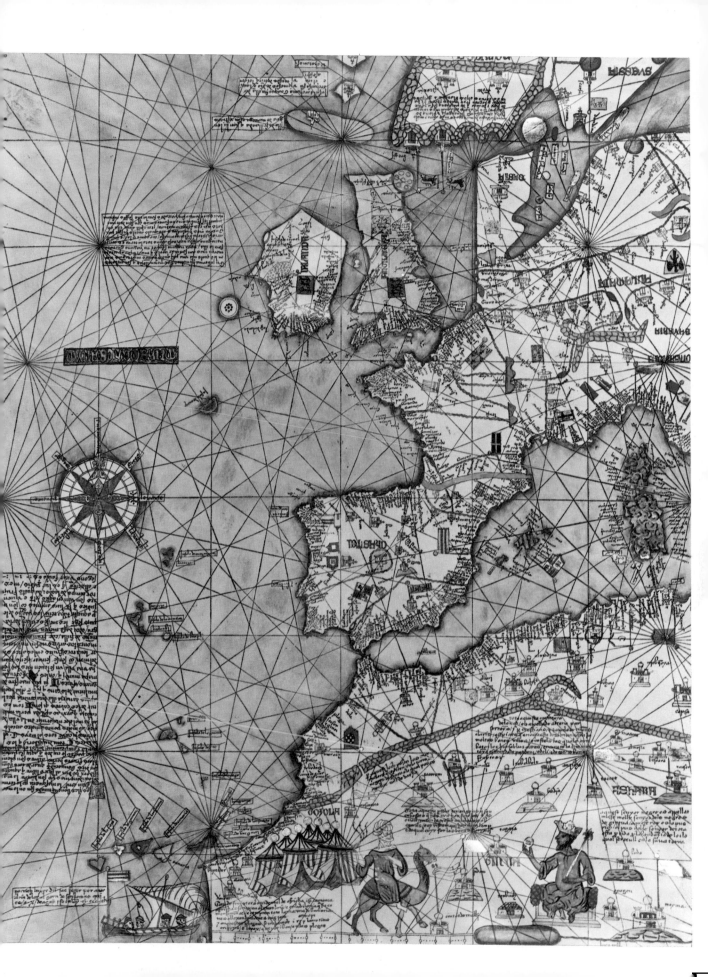

There is some evidence, though no certainty, that even at this time, Henry envisaged a direct sea route to the East.

It was soon after returning from a second stay in Ceuta, in 1418, that Henry resolved to begin a program of systematic and purposeful exploration. He did not intend to become an explorer himself. As he saw it, his role was to plan and supervise the program—to choose, train, and encourage promising sea captains and pilots, and to analyze and interpret the results of their expeditions. With this plan in mind, Henry gave up court life—though he always remained ready to serve as statesman or soldier when his country so required. He took up residence near the port of Lagos, and prepared himself for what was to be his life's work by a diligent study of mathematics, astronomy, and geography.

A few miles from Lagos, at the extreme southwestern tip of Portugal, stood Sagres, a small, bleak promontory pointing toward the African coast. There, in time, Henry built an observatory, a fortress, a naval arsenal, and a small town. There too, he established what we have come to call his "school of navigation."

Little is known about this institution, for the Portuguese were almost as secretive about their ocean voyages as the Phoenicians had been before them. All that is certain is that at Sagres pilots were chosen, given their instructions and some form of training, and sent on their way. It has also been established that Henry had the services of an expert on nautical instruments and mapmaking, a certain Master Jacome of Majorca. Master Jacome was employed by Henry to update charts

Above: Henry the Navigator's connection with Sagres began when he was made governor of Algarve, Portugal's southernmost province, and his private chapel can still be seen. On the site now occupied by a lighthouse, he built a navigational school and observatory.

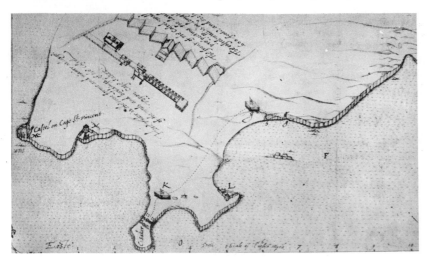

Left: this drawing from the 1500's shows about 11 miles around Sagres, where Prince Henry built a naval arsenal and fortress as well as his famous school of navigation.

of the African coast and the Atlantic islands as each voyage of discovery brought back new information.

But even so accomplished a cartographer as Master Jacome must have been very limited in the help he could give to Henry's pilots. For at that time mapmaking was anything but an exact science, and the few navigational instruments were still very primitive.

There were no accurate instruments for determining a ship's position and direction. Much of the time the early mariners had to sail out of sight of land to avoid the danger of being blown onto the coast by strong on-shore winds. Although the north-seeking properties of magnets had been known for centuries, nothing was yet known about magnetic variation and deviation. As a result, the most advanced instrument in use—the mariner's compass—could be very misleading. Out of sight of land, therefore, Henry's pilots had to rely heavily on

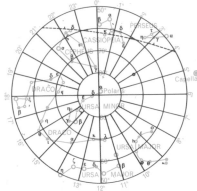

Above: Henry's pilots' most accurate aid to navigation was a knowledge of the stars. North of the equator they judged direction from the Pole Star. Below: the astrolabe was used to measure the positions of the stars.

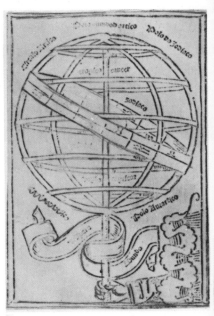

Left: this compass in an ivory box dates from about 1500. There is no definite record as to who first used a compass, but pieces of magnetic iron had been used since the 1000's to guide ships within sight of land.

their knowledge of the heavens to determine their changing position and direction.

By night, so long as they remained north of the equator, pilots could see the Pole Star, which they knew always lay very close to true north. By day, so long as they remained north of the Tropic of Cancer, the sun would always be due south at noon. And it would be 15° farther to the east for each hour nearer to sunrise, and 15° farther to the west for each hour nearer to sunset. To tell the hour during the day, mariners depended on the sun. The shadow of a stick set upright on deck grew shorter as morning wore on, longer again as afternoon moved toward sunset. The moment when the shadow was at its shortest marked true noon. By night, pilots could tell the time from the changing position of the stars in the constellation Ursa Minor.

To determine the ship's position was even more difficult than establishing the ship's direction. And it was, of course, just as difficult to determine the exact position of newly-discovered capes, islands, and river mouths. The discovery of Ptolemy's *Geography* a few years before Henry's program of exploration began, led to fresh thinking. As a result of this work, learned mapmakers such as Master Jacome had begun to realize that the ideal way of fixing a ship's position was in terms of latitude and longitude. But this was no easy matter in the 1400's.

To determine longitude at sea it is necessary to know, precisely and simultaneously, both local time and the time at some other fixed point, such as the home port. There was no simple method of ascertaining these two times at once until the 1700's when the marine chronometer was invented. In the meantime, pilots attempting to fix longitude had to use Ptolemy's rough estimate of the east-west distance represented by one degree of longitude along each parallel of latitude. This meant that they had to keep track of how far east or west they traveled on each stage of their voyage. To do this, they noted the direction in which they were sailing, how long they had sailed in that direction, and the speed at which they had traveled. Speed could be assessed by throwing some floating object overboard from the ship's prow and noting how long the vessel (whose length was known) took to pass it.

Latitude could be determined (in theory at least) by measuring the angular distance of the Pole Star above the horizon. Land-based astronomers had long been able to take such measurements quite accurately with the aid of a sophisticated instrument of Arab invention called the astrolabe. But the astronomer's astrolabe was useless on the heaving

Above: an hourglass was important to early mariners, as mechanical clocks were unreliable at sea. Time measurement was an important element in "dead reckoning," by which the early pilot worked out the ship's position.

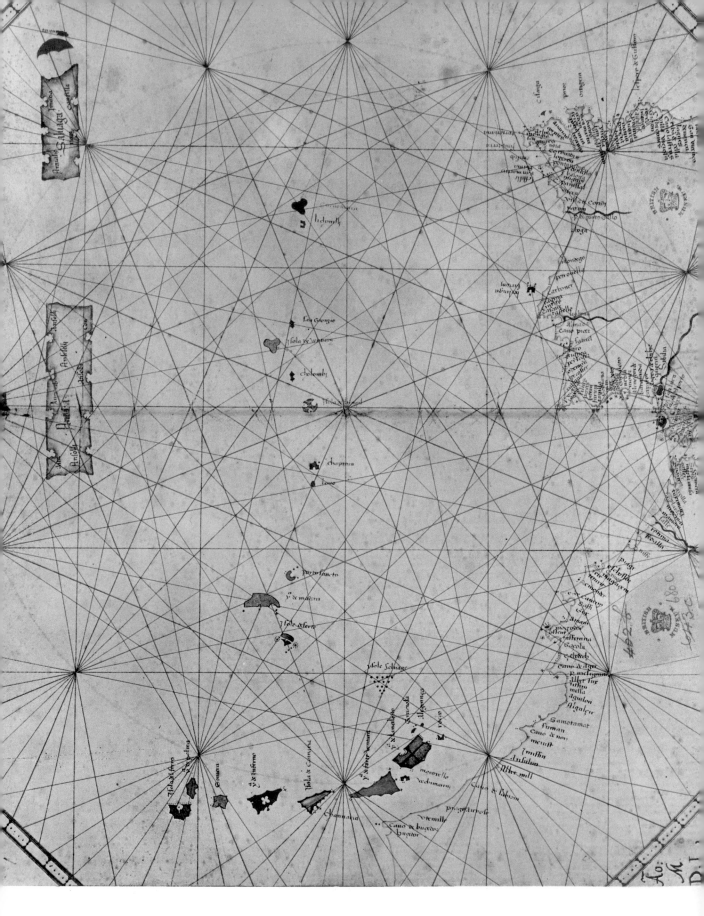

deck of a ship at sea. The quadrant was a simpler instrument that could also be used for angular measurement. But it was not, so far as is known, employed by Portuguese pilots until a year or two before Prince Henry's death. Instead, an even simpler "instrument" was used—the pilot's hand! When attempting to fix latitude, most pilots measured the height of the Pole Star above the horizon simply by stretching out a hand at arm's length. If the space between horizon and star was blocked out by the thickness of a finger, the star's angle above the horizon was about $2°$; if blocked out by the thickness of the wrist, about $8°$; if blocked out by the full span of the hand, about $18°$.

The rough and ready results obtained by these methods made it impossible for cartographers to indicate exact location by reference to latitude and longitude. Indeed, until well into the 1500's, maps of the African coast were usually plotted on the same kind of complicated chart that had been used by Mediterranean mariners since the last of the Crusades. Such charts were drawn on a grid consisting of many criss-crossing lines. These radiated from two or more compass points near the edges of the chart and indicated compass bearings. With the help of a ruler and a pair of dividers, the pilot could determine which grid line was most nearly parallel to the course between his present position and the harbor he was seeking. Then, by tracing that line to the compass point from which it radiated, he could discover which compass bearing he would need to follow.

Thus, when Prince Henry sent forth his first ships, navigational instruments were barely adequate to the needs of ocean explorers. And maps and cartographic devices were only slightly better at recording their discoveries. But Prince Henry had at his command two very important assets—good ships and competent men.

Coincidentally, it was just about the time of Henry's first explorative mission that a new type of ship, the caravel, was coming into use. Though light, the caravel was broad of beam and capable of carrying a good supply of water and provisions. In addition, these seaworthy vessels often had two types of sails: triangular lateen sails for tacking and making full use of light and side winds, and square sails for moving fast before a following wind.

More important still to Henry's program was the availability of many brave and experienced seamen. The prince was to make wise use of these resourceful men in the great campaign of discovery and exploration he now undertook.

Above: typical of the Portuguese ships which Henry sent out, this ship has square-rigged sails and normal lateen construction, by which a long yard suspends the sails from the mast.

Sea of Darkness
3

Prince Henry began his campaign of exploration with high hopes. He fully expected his mariners would soon be sailing down the coast of Africa and returning with the news he longed to hear: that the coast had been thoroughly explored and charted; that a substantial number of non-Christians had been converted to the true faith; and that valuable new trading contacts had been established. But the prince was to be kept waiting many years for even a partial fulfillment of his dreams, mainly because of the fearsome stories then prevailing about the "Sea of Darkness." This became particularly evident when the exploration involved sailing into the unknown seas beyond the Ca-

Above: in the 1400's and 1500's, Portuguese navigators explored up and down the coast of Africa, establishing colonies and trading stations. At first fear of the unknown was stronger than their obedience to Prince Henry and all his exhortations to sail south of Cape Bojador failed. However, this bulge (which now appears to us quite insignificant) was eventually rounded and the myth of boiling seas and waterless land exploded. Portuguese exploration flourished, leading eventually to circumnavigation of the African continent.

Above: in this day and age dress had not yet become specialized and uniform was unknown. This ship's captain is wearing the same type of clothes as any reasonably well-to-do gentleman of the period and he would wear the same whether on his ship or on land.

nary Islands, which lay 800 miles southwest of Portugal. And Henry's mariners were still less eager to venture past Cape Bojador, a small bulge of land on the coast of the present-day Spanish Sahara, some 150 miles south of the Canaries. No one, to their knowledge, had ever sailed past Bojador and returned to tell the tale. Keen and well-trained as Henry's mariners were, they were loath to risk their necks for the sake of mere exploration.

The stories that abounded about the seas beyond Cape Bojador were enough to make even the stoutest hearts quail. Some had it that beyond Bojador the ocean boiled and steamed. Others stated flatly that "beyond this cape there is no population, no water, neither trees nor green herbs; and the sea is so shallow that a league [a unit of distance varying between three and four miles] from the shore its depth is hardly a fathom. The tides are so strong that any ship which passes the cape will never be able to return." It is small wonder then that Henry's seamen asked themselves, "How shall we pass beyond the limits established by our elders? What profit can the prince win from the loss of our souls and our bodies?"

So, for some 15 years, instead of following Henry's instructions to pursue a steady course south beyond Cape Bojador, his mariners would veer off in other directions and go crusading or trading. Some sailed east into the Mediterranean to raid Moslem-held Granada on the southern coast of the Iberian Peninsula. Others sailed even farther east to the lands at the other end of the Mediterranean, where they devoted themselves to the capture of infidels.

How did the prince react to the news that his orders had been completely disregarded? Henry was a patient man—perhaps too patient. Instead of reprimanding his reluctant explorers, he rewarded them for their crusading efforts.

Meanwhile, some of Henry's mariners—either acting on instructions, or seeking yet another way to avoid going past Cape Bojador—were making more useful excursions. These captains sailed westward into the Atlantic. They took their ships and crews to the Canary Islands, the Madeira Islands, and the Azores. As a result of their journeys, Portugal became the first nation to use these islands for the purposes of regular trade and colonization. Eventually the Canaries and Madeiras became ports of call for ships en route to more distant lands.

All three archipelagos had been known to Europeans for centuries. As far back as the A.D. 100's, Ptolemy had mentioned the Canaries,

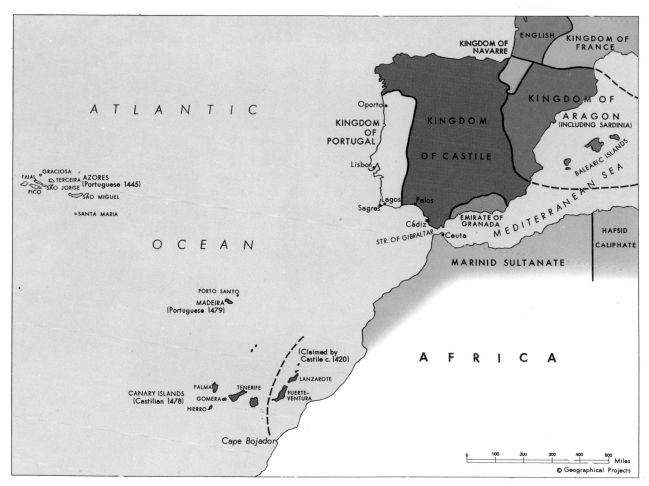

calling them the Fortunate Isles. Since then, the Canary Islands had been visited from time to time by sailors from the Moslem Empire, Genoa, Normandy, Castile, and Portugal. By the time Prince Henry's explorations began, Castile had already staked a claim to the two islands nearest the African coast, Lanzarote and Fuerteventura. The outer islands, however, remained virtually unexplored. Realizing their potential as springboards for future African exploration, Henry determined to take possession of these islands.

In 1425, he sent a fleet carrying more than 2,000 men and 100 horses to conquer the outer island of Gran Canaria, and in 1427, he sent another fleet on the same mission. Both expeditions, hampered by inadequate

Above: Portugal and Castile, just before Ferdinand and Isabella expelled the Moors from Granada, showing the Azores, Madeira, and the Canary Islands.

45

provisions, failed to overcome the stubborn resistance of the natives. But efforts to take the outer islands were renewed from time to time, and Portugal soon made enough headway to worry the Castilians.

In 1435, Castile and Portugal asked the pope to settle the question of possession of the Canaries. His decision, given in 1436, was that Castile should retain Lanzarote and Fuerteventura, while Portugal should have a free hand in the outer islands of Gran Canaria, Tenerife, Palma, and Gomera. Much later, in 1479, Spanish sovereignty over the Canaries was finally established by the treaty of Alcacova between Portugal and Castile. However, while Portugal retained her right to the outer isles, her sailors made good use of them as bases for replenishing their drinking water and food supplies on long voyages.

Oddly enough, the sister islands of Madeira and Porto Santo had never yet been claimed, despite the fact that they lay closer to Europe than the Canaries. During the first years of Henry's exploration program they became Portuguese possessions almost by accident.

As early at 1418, Henry had fitted out a ship for two of his young squires, João Gonçalves Zarco and Tristan Vaz Teixeira, and instructed them to sail south along the African coast beyond Cape Bojador, until they came to Guinea. Zarco and Teixeira had not sailed far before

Left: Gran Canaria, the most fertile of the Canary Islands (known to Ptolemy as the Fortunate Islands) in the Atlantic 60 miles northwest of the African coast. It was to Gran Canaria that Prince Henry turned his attention in the early 1400's when two expeditions sent by him tried to gain control of the island. A decree by the pope in 1436 gave Portugal control of the outer islands, among them Gran Canaria, and they made good use of bases set up there. Their control lasted until Spain took over all the islands in the late 1400's.

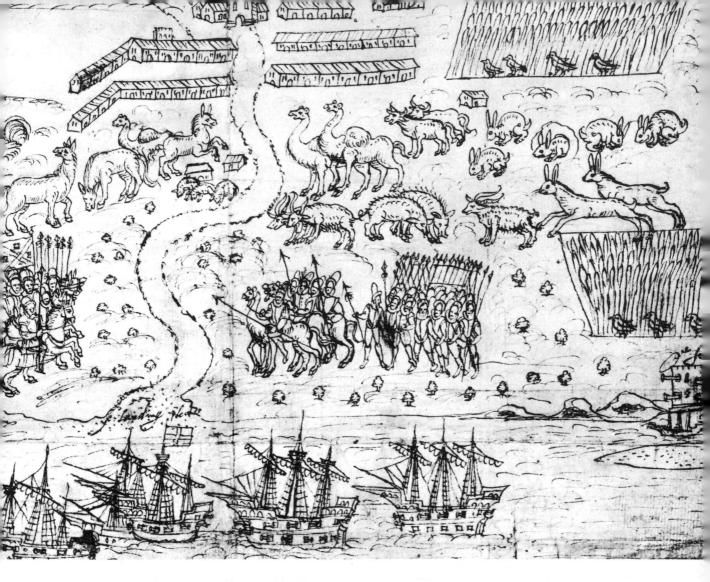

they met with contrary winds. They had to do a good deal of tacking to make any headway, and in the course of their maneuvers, sighted Porto Santo. Landing there, they decided that the island was well suited for colonization, and sailed back to Sagres immediately to report the good news.

Henry was pleased with their report and at once sent some colonists to Porto Santo. Unfortunately, however, one of them took along a pregnant rabbit. Its first offspring multiplied many times very quickly, and soon multitudes of hungry rabbits were eating up everything the colonists planted. In the end, the settlers had to abandon Porto Santo and transfer to Madeira some 12 leagues distant—this time without rabbits! Madeira's abundant sunshine and water made crops flourish, particularly sugar cane and grapes, and the islanders soon prospered as exporters of wine and sugar.

The Azores, like the Canaries, had been discovered centuries before, although no one knows exactly when or by whom. Certainly their positions had been plotted (albeit inaccurately) on the Laurentian Portolan, a map made in 1381. However, like Madeira and Porto Santo,

Above: the island of Lanzarote, the most easterly of the Canary Islands, from an old manuscript drawing of about 1590. Lanzarote and Fuerteventura remained under Castilian rule by the pope's decree of 1436. Mountainous and barren, and of volcanic origin, the island is about 31 miles long and 5 to 10 miles in width.

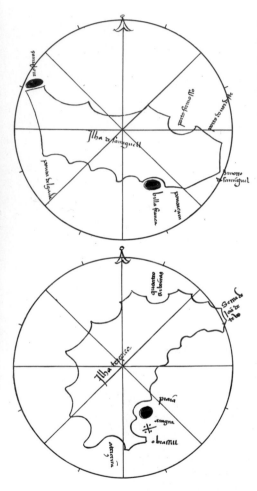

Above: an early map of the Azores, showing the islands of Terciera and Samiguell, from Cartas de Valentim Fernandes 1506—1508. While the rough shape of the islands is correct, the mapmaker has made no attempt to make a detailed outline of the coast. The Azores, which were colonized by Portugal in the mid-1400's, are the remotest group of any of the Atlantic islands, the nearest continental land—800 miles east of Samiguell—being Cape da Roca in Portugal. The islands became a rendezvous for fleets on their voyages from the Indies.

the Azores were first colonized by the Portuguese. In 1431, Henry sent Gonçalo Cabral to sail westward in search of islands he believed must exist. Cabral was unsuccessful, but the following year he reached an island which he named St. Mary. Twelve years later, Henry, upon hearing reports of a larger island, commissioned Cabral to set out again. As a result of this voyage the island of St. Michael was discovered in 1444, and the first Portuguese settlers arrived there about 1445. The Azores never achieved the same economic importance as Madeira. They were, however, very useful havens for Portuguese vessels returning from South Africa, because the trade winds made the detour to the Azores the easiest way home.

On the credit side, then, the first years of Henry's exploration program had produced some satisfactory results. His men had struck a number of minor blows against Moslem power in the Mediterranean. They had colonized Madeira and staked a claim to the Azores. They were close to taking several of the Canary Islands. *But they had not yet ventured beyond Cape Bojador.* In this, the first step in Henry's exploration program, his mariners had produced no results at all. Henry's patience, like his money, was fast running out.

In the year 1433, the prince placed one of his squires, Gil Eannes, in command of a barca, and once again gave the order to proceed as far as possible down the African coast. The squire set out bravely, but, in the end, he "made the same voyage as the others had made and, overcome by the same dread, did not pass beyond the Canary Islands." On his return, Eannes unwisely excused his failure by detailing the extreme perils he had been warned about by other seamen. At this, Henry's patience finally gave out. "In truth, I marvel at these imaginings which have possessed you all," he said. "If these things possessed any authority, however small, I might still find excuse for you. But I am astonished that you accept them from the opinion of mariners who know only the navigation of Flanders, and cannot handle a compass or a chart of the seas."

With this, Henry sent Eannes out to try again, and the good squire "promised himself resolutely that he would never again appear before his lord without having accomplished the mission charged upon him."

This resolution must have stood him in good stead. For in 1434 Eannes returned with the joyful news that he had succeeded in rounding Cape Bojador. He had landed just beyond it and gathered a few plants—St. Mary's roses—to show the prince what grew there.

Above: Gabo Girão, a lofty headland stretching out into the sea from Madeira, the larger of the two inhabited islands in the Funchal group in the North Atlantic, about 360 miles from the African coast. Madeira was colonized by Henry the Navigator and much of the island brought under cultivation. A thriving trade in Madeiran sugar was soon started.

Below: Hull evolution 1400—1600. On the left is a carrack with consolidated forecastle and raking guns in round open ports. This later developed, as on the right, with two counters aft, a heavy forecastle with boomkins (spurs on either side of the bow holding the foresail foretack) beneath. Its guns are in rectangular ports furnished with lids.

Right: Resurrection plant (Anastatica hierochuntina), the "St. Mary's rose" found by Gil Eannes when he landed after succeeding in rounding the dreaded Cape Bojador in 1433.
A member of the mustard family, during the dry season the mature plant loses its leaves and the stem curls into a ball with the seed pod inside. This is blown about by the wind, like a tumbleweed, until the rainy season. When wet the plants unfold and the branches spread out and turn green.

In general, his voyage had been calm and uneventful, and "he had found matters very different from what he and others had imagined."

If we think only in terms of geography, Eannes' voyage had accomplished little, for Cape Bojador is only 150 miles south of the Canaries. The value of his voyage, however, lay not in passing a particular cape, but in surmounting a barrier of fear. For centuries, sailors had thought of the seas south of Bojador as a waste of waters fraught with horror and disaster. To them, the sea there was aptly described by the Arab term for it— "the Sea of Darkness."

Eannes, whose voyage had done so much to dispel man's fears, received a knighthood. Now many other seamen came forward and declared they were ready to go farther than Eannes.

Left: monk seals found along the northwest coast of Africa. Baldaya took seals back to Portugal from an expedition 500 miles south of Cape Bojador. He had previously seen footprints in the area, so Prince Henry sent him back to speak with, and possibly to capture, some of the inhabitants. Baldaya failed to make contact with a group of people that he saw, so he killed and collected the seals to make up for his failure.

Prince Henry knew that Eannes' success marked the long awaited turning point in his campaign. This opinion was supported by his elder brother Edward, who had become king on the death of their father in the summer of 1433. As proof of his faith in the future of his brother's program, Edward improved Henry's financial position by making over to him the "royal fifth" of all profits accruing from Madeira's fast-growing export trade.

In 1435 Henry dispatched another expedition, consisting of a barinel captained by Alfonso Gonçalves Baldaya, and a caravel captained by Gil Eannes. The two ships sailed 200 miles beyond Cape Bojador, and brought back the news that, on landing, the crew had seen the tracks of men and camels.

When Baldaya reported this to the prince, Henry said, "Since you have found these footprints, it seems to me that there must be some population not far off, or perchance there are people who go there with merchandise for some seaport. Thus I intend to send you again in the same barinel; and I charge you to do your best to contrive to speak with these people, or capture some of them so that I may receive intelligence of their land."

It was probably in 1436 that Baldaya and his small crew set out again. This time Baldaya sailed almost 100 miles beyond Bojador before landing near an inlet which he mistook for a river mouth. Here he dispatched two youths, mounted on the horses they had brought with them, and armed, to look for local inhabitants or traders. They had ridden several miles along the shore when they suddenly spotted a group of 19 men armed with spears. Thinking that the men would be at a disadvantage because they were not on horseback, the two youths set upon the group in an attempt to take prisoners. In the fray that followed, they not only failed to take captives, but barely escaped with their lives. They managed to get away and reach the coast, where they reported to Baldaya. The next day, he and a few others returned to the place where the armed men had been seen, but the natives had disappeared.

Baldaya had failed in his mission to "speak with these people or capture some of them," or to discover "whether they were Moors or Gentiles or what was their manner of living." But before returning, he did what he could to make up for it. On a sandbank near where his barinel lay at anchor there were thousands of large seals. He and his men killed as many as they could and loaded their ship with the skins. This

Above: three short stabbing spears of the type used by African tribes. The center one was merely for ceremonial use, but the others were actual weapons used against the Portuguese invaders.

Above: Prince Ferdinand of Portugal,
Henry's youngest brother. When the
Portuguese attack on Tangier in 1437
failed, Ferdinand had to be left
behind as a hostage. He died six
years later, still a Moslem prisoner.

was to be the first cargo of commercial value to reach Portugal from the bulge of Africa. Before returning home, Baldaya sailed another 100 miles southwest and reached the narrow bay that was later named Río de Oro—river of gold. Baldaya did not know it, but he was within striking distance of the gold-bearing area regularly visited by Arab caravans.

When Baldaya finally reached home with his cargo of sealskins, it seemed that the time had come at last for a full-scale program of exploration, and the realization of Henry's hopes. But just at this moment, an ill-conceived attempt to repeat the success of the Ceuta episode played havoc with the fortunes of Portugal in general and of the royal family in particular.

Henry's younger brother Ferdinand (Fernando), now 34, was impatient to be knighted on the field of battle. He therefore urged King Edward to mount an attack on the northern African port of Tangier, a Moslem stronghold about 40 miles west of Ceuta. Somewhat reluctantly, Edward agreed and launched the attack in August, 1437, with Prince Henry leading the army.

The expedition failed disastrously and the Portuguese were allowed to escape with their lives only by promising to restore Ceuta to the Moslems. Furthermore, they were compelled to leave Prince Ferdinand behind as a guarantee of good faith. In the end, Ceuta was not returned to the Moslems. The Church maintained—as, of course, Henry did—that a Christian city (and Ceuta was now officially a Christian city) belonged to God and could not be handed over to infidels. As a result, the luckless Prince Ferdinand had to be left in Moslem hands. He died, still a Moslem prisoner, some six years later. In the meantime, King Edward, who had for a long time been in poor health and was now tortured by remorse over the fate of his brother, worried himself into an early grave.

In September, 1438, when Edward died, his son and heir, Alfonso, was still a child. The question of whether his mother or his eldest uncle, Peter, should be regent until Alfonso came of age brought Portugal to the verge of civil war. Prince Henry played a leading role in the delicate diplomatic maneuvers which eventually restored an atmosphere of calm under the regency of Prince Peter. But not until the matter was finally settled, in 1441, could Henry give his attention once more to exploration.

In that year he sent out a small vessel under the command of one Antão

Os montes craros em a sr

Caste lodamina

Above: a thriving trade in human beings was set up in the mid-1400's when at last Prince Henry's explorers rounded the fearful Cape Bojador. Expeditions from 1441 on brought back captives, from whom Prince Henry tried to find out about their country, and whom he tried, with moderate success, to convert to Christianity. Others, however, saw the captives only as the basis of a lucrative slave trade, and more and more expeditions were undertaken for the sole purpose of bringing slaves to the Lagos markets.

Gonçalves, and an armed caravel under the command of a knight, Nuno Tristão. Because Gonçalves was very young, he was simply asked to go as far as he could and return with a cargo of sealskins and seal oil. Tristão, accompanied by one of Henry's Moorish servants to act as interpreter, was instructed to bring back natives of the African coast who might be able to provide useful geographical information. Gonçalves reached a point just south of the Río de Oro and quickly collected his cargo. Then, on his own initiative, he decided to take a few captives. With nine crew members he marched inland, and, after several skirmishes, managed to take two prisoners: a Berber of the Azenegue tribe, and a Negro slave who belonged to the Azenegues.

By then, Tristão's caravel had reached the same spot. The two crews joined forces in a second inland raid. This time, after surrounding two small camps of natives, they took 10 more captives, including a chief named Adahu, who had traveled more than his fellows and could speak the Moorish tongue. We are told that, from Adahu, Prince Henry later obtained "intelligence of a great measure of the affairs of the region which he inhabited." Gonçalves now returned to Portugal, while Tristão, in an unsuccessful attempt to take more captives, sailed farther on to Cape Blanc, a point about 250 miles south of the Río de Oro.

Prince Henry regarded the 12 captives primarily as sources of information and as souls to be saved. But other men in Portugal saw them in terms of potential profit. To such men, the capture of these people heralded the opening of a lucrative slave trade. As a result, however lofty Prince Henry's motives remained, more and more of his captains took advantage of their sailing orders to raid the African coast for slaves and cheap-bought cargoes. Some genuine exploration still went on, but it usually took second place to these more mercenary objectives.

The regent, Prince Peter, certainly realized that African exploration now appeared capable of paying dividends. Knowing how much Henry had already spent on fostering African exploration, Peter made over to him the "royal fifth" of all profits it might bring in. He also decreed that no ship was to sail beyond Cape Bojador without Henry's permission.

In 1442, Gonçalves made a second voyage. With him he took Chief Adahu and two of the other Azenegue captives, hoping to exchange them for a greater number of the Azenegues' Negro slaves. He succeeded, and returned home with 10 slaves, as well as a little gold dust and many ostrich eggs. But he had not advanced the cause of exploration at all, having sailed no farther than the Río de Oro.

The following year, Nuno Tristão did sail about 100 miles beyond Cape Blanc to a bay, in present-day Mauritania, in which he discovered the island of Arguim. (Here the Portuguese soon afterward established their first permanent trading station in tropical Africa.) At Arguim he took 28 captives and promptly set sail for home, "more joyous than the first time because the take was greater, and also because he was alone and had no need to share it."

When Tristão returned, he landed at the port of Lagos. The report of his success soon reached the ears of the city's treasurer, a man called Lançarote. Seeing the chance for a profitable investment, Lançarote, with Henry's permission, equipped and manned six caravels and set off to duplicate Tristão's voyage. In and around Arguim and its adjacent islands—Tider and the Isle of Herons—he and his crew captured more than 200 men, women, and children, who were brought back to Lagos and sold at public auction. Azurara reports with pride that most

Above: an ostrich chick breaking out of an egg. Ostriches are the largest living birds—the male can be as tall as 8 feet, and can weigh 345 pounds. The female lays as many as 10 eggs in a clutch and these are of equally mammoth proportions. Nearly six inches in diameter, weighing about three pounds, they have a thick shell and are a dull yellow color. Antão Gonçalves took several ostrich eggs back with him from Cape Blanc.

Left: a young Arab boy holding a goat. For many centuries before the arrival of the Portuguese invaders, nomadic Arab tribes had wandered through the African continent spreading the word of Islam by conquest.
Below: Lagos, seaport of southern Portugal. It was here that Prince Henry established the town of Sagres, near Cape St. Vincent. In the 1440's, Lagos became the center of the slave trade, where captives from the islands around Cape Blanc were auctioned.

of them were well treated and later became good Christians, but he spares none of the grim details in describing the agonizing scenes at the auction as husbands were parted from their wives, and children from their mothers.

Despite the growing Portuguese interest in slaving, Henry himself continued to press for exploration. He now equipped a caravel for Gonçalo de Sintra, a man reared from childhood in his own household, and urged him to concentrate on discovery and on nothing else. Near

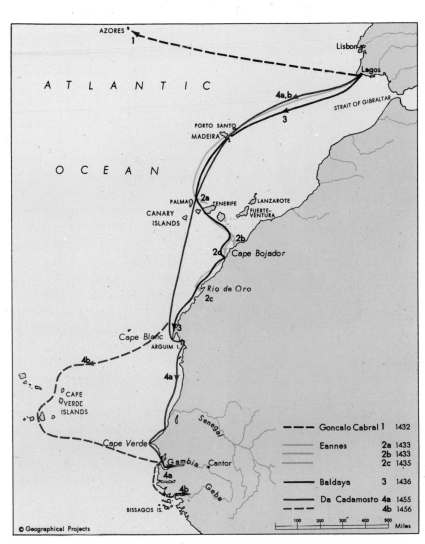

Above: the routes of the Portuguese explorers during the mid-1400's, west to the Azores, and southwest through the Canary Islands and down the west coast of Africa.

Cape Blanc, however, De Sintra was tempted to try his hand at slaving. But the people of this region had learned from the fate of their hapless neighbors to beware of white men. Turning on the would-be slavers, they killed De Sintra and seven of his companions.

In the same year (1444), several vessels set out from Portugal with the laudable purpose of arranging a treaty of trade with the Azenegues. The attempt failed—again because previous Portuguese visits had taught the people to distrust white men. The expedition did have one

Above: the use of feathers and paint by the Africans led the Portuguese to conclude that these people, whose customs, behavior, and dress were so different from their own, were uncivilized, primitive, and childlike.

notable result, however. One of the crew, João Fernandes, who understood the language of the Moors, requested that he be left behind to live among the people and learn their ways. After staying with the Moors and their Berber and Tuareg neighbors for several months, he returned to Portugal and gave an informative report to the prince.

Thereafter, several expeditions did venture much farther south—if only because it was easier to capture slaves where the white man's reputation had not preceded him. But, in general, exploration for its own sake continued to take a back seat to slave trading.

In 1445, on his third voyage, Nuno Tristão sailed far beyond Arguim Island, past the end of the desert coast, and reached a shore "where there were many palms and other trees, and all the fields looked to be fertile." Here Tristão took 21 captives before he set sail for home. Some months later, an elderly man named Dinis Dias, who had turned explorer because "he was unwilling to let himself grow soft in the well-being of repose," set a new record by sailing some 500 miles south of Cape Blanc and reaching the most westerly point in all Africa. This point (the site of present-day Dakar, in Senegal), he named Cape Verde. Perhaps the success of Dias' voyage owed something to the fact that he contented himself with taking only four captives.

During the next three years, there were numerous other expeditions, one of which consisted of a great fleet of 26 vessels from Lagos, Lisbon, and Madeira. But few captains who set out from Portugal during this period sailed farther south than had old Dinis Dias. In 1446, however, Nuno Tristão succeeded in reaching a point about 200 miles south of Cape Verde. Here he met his death in a slave raid. But on this, his last voyage, he had reached the shores of Guinea. Later in 1446, a man named Álvaro Fernandes sailed some 500 miles beyond Cape Verde, reaching the area now occupied by Sierra Leone.

Although there were other voyages down the African coast during the next two years, no further progress had been made by the end of 1448, when Azurara brought his *Chronicle of the Discovery of Guinea* to a close. The *Chronicle* had been commissioned by King Alfonso V and scrutinized by Prince Henry himself, and in all probability its coming to a stop in 1448 was because civil war broke out. This caused a second major pause in Portuguese exploration. In any event, Guinea had at long last been reached, and possibly Azurara believed that "what came to pass afterward did not call for such effort and fatigue" as had been required in pioneering the first 1,500 miles of coastline beyond Bojador.

South to Hope

4

The cause of the civil war, which brought exploration to a halt, arose from a quarrel between the young Alfonso V and his uncle Peter, the former regent. Prince Peter was defeated and killed on the field of battle in May, 1449.

Prince Henry, torn between love for his brother and loyalty to his nephew, the king, had taken no part in the fighting. Nevertheless, it had been impossible for him to devote his energies to exploration until peace was restored.

Then another hindrance to Portuguese exploration presented itself. This was the continuing trouble (despite the pope's decision of 1436) with Castile over possession of the Canaries. Between 1450 and 1455 the two nations were frequently on the brink of war over this issue. During this time, many of Henry's ships were needed in the vicinity

of the Canaries to protect Portuguese interests there. As a result, he had few ships available for voyages of discovery.

With the conclusion of hostilities between Portugal and Castile, Portuguese exploration seems to have sprung to life once more—although at first in a small way. Certainly, Portuguese ships began visiting the African coast in ever-increasing numbers. Among the mariners of this period was Alvise da Cadamosto, a Venetian sea trader who entered Prince Henry's service in 1455 and who later wrote a full account of his experiences. His narrative, although it records no great discoveries, tells us much about what had so far been achieved by Portugal in the way of exploration and colonization. It also gives us a vivid description at first-hand of what it was like to be one of Prince Henry's mariners.

Cadamosto first took to sea trading in an effort to restore the lost

Above: ladies and gentlemen of the Portuguese court, showing the elaborate style of dress fashionable in the 1500's. One of the difficulties that explorers had to face was that their orders came from a center of culture and luxury and may not always have been relevant to the rough and ready conditions of the explorers. But the captains under Henry the Navigator were fortunate, as the prince apparently kept himself aware of the circumstances of his men and was sympathetic to their needs.

Above: Alfonso V succeeded his father, Edward, when only six years old. He was under the regency of his mother and then of his uncle, Peter, whose daughter he married. After assuming control in 1448, he was misled into believing Peter to be a rebel and Peter was killed at the ensuing battle of Alfarrobeira. Alfonsó successfully invaded Moorish Africa and became known as "Alfonso the African."

fortunes of his family. He had already visited lands as far apart as Egypt and the Netherlands when, in 1454, he set sail with a trading fleet bound for Flanders which made a stop in southern Portugal. While there, Cadamosto learned of the profitable voyages being made by Portuguese seamen, and saw some of the valuable cargoes they were bringing back from Madeira and Guinea. He made inquiries, and found that a foreigner could participate in this trade if he obtained Henry's permission and accepted his terms.

Having obtained the necessary permission, Cadamosto immediately abandoned the Venetain fleet to enter Henry's service. The prince offered an adventurous man every chance of making money with no financial risk to himself. Henry would provide him with a caravel and goods to trade free of charge. In return, he was to sail as far as he found reasonable and return with as much valuable cargo as possible. The profit from the sale of the cargo would be divided equally between the prince and himself. If there should be no profit—and even if there should be no cargo to speak of—Henry had agreed to stand the loss.

Cadamosto set out on his first voyage for the prince on March 22, 1455. In three days he had reached Porto Santo, and in six, Madeira. Although he did not stay long at either, he had much to report about both. Porto Santo, he found, had by now been successfully colonized, and the settlers there were prospering by raising cattle and exporting quantities of honey and wax. In Madeira, there were now four settlements. Besides producing wine and sugar for export, they were growing wheat, cutting timber, manufacturing furniture, and raising cattle.

Cadamosto then called in at Gomera and Ferro in the Canaries. Here he learned that, as in the neighboring islands of Lanzarote and Fuerteventura, most of the natives had been converted to Christianity.

But it was about the African coast that Cadamosto had most to report. At Cape Blanc, he learned of the caravan route between the north coast of Africa and Timbuktu (a city in present-day Mali). Moslem traders from northern Africa traveled south along this route carrying articles of brass and silver which they traded at Timbuktu for gold, pepper, and slaves. Cadamosto discovered, however, that already the volume of trade along this overland route had been noticeably affected by the Portuguese sea trade. Coastal goods that had once been available only to overland merchants were now being bought by Portuguese traders and shipped to Lisbon.

PRIMO

In comenza el libro de la prima Nauigatione per loeceano a le terre de Nigri de la Bafla Ethiopia per comandamento del Illuft. Signor Infante Don Hurich fratello de Don Dourth Re de Portogallo.

El primo che ha trouato la nauigation del mare occeano uerfo el mezodi. c.i.

Sſendo lo Alouife da Ca da mo fto ſtato el primo:ch delanation de la nobel Cita de Venefia ſi adimoſſo an auigare el mare occeano di fori del ſtretto de zibeltera uerfo le pte demezodi in leterre de Nigri dla bafla Ethiopia. doue i qſto mio iti nerario hauendo uiſto moke cofe noue : & degne de qualche noto: acioche quelli che de mi haueráno adiſcendere poflino itendere ʠllo fia ſtato lo aɪo mio ɪn hauer mefſo accerchare uarie cofe in diuerſi & noui lochɪ:che ueramɐte & icoſtumi: & lilochi nrɪ in cóparatió dela cofa per me ueduta & inteſa:uno altro mondo fe poteria chiamare: de qua e adunqua ʠceſſo:che benemerito farne qualche nota.che come lamemoria me feruira: cufi có la pɐna tranſcorero le cofe pdiɛte:le quale fe p mɪ nó feráno cufi ordinatamente mefʃe :come lamateria richiede:almeno nó manchero de itegra uerita in ogni pte:& queſto fenza dubio piu pſto de mancho dicendo:che ultra el uero alcuna cofa narrando.Adúqua e da fapere:che ʠlui che fu el primo Inuɛtore de far nauigar ʠſta pte del mare occeáo uer

a

Farther south, at the island of Arguim, Cadamosto saw the fort that had been erected on Henry's instructions to protect Portuguese trade. Here at Arguim, he learned, only licensed and resident Portuguese merchants were allowed to trade directly with the Arabs. In exchange for such goods as wheat and cloth, which were brought south from Portugal in Henry's ships, merchants obtained a considerable quantity of gold, and as many as 1,000 Negro slaves each year. Henry apparently hoped that slaves purchased from the Arabs would later convert to Christianity more readily than slaves that had been captured from their villages by raiders who were professed Christians.

From Arguim, Cadamosto pushed on to the Senegal River, which meets the sea about 100 miles north of Cape Verde. The Portuguese had already established trade relations with the people of this area and, at a spot some 50 miles farther on, Cadamosto decided to do some trading

of his own. In negotiations with a chief named Budomel, he traded
Spanish horses, woolen cloth, and Moorish silk for slaves.

From Cadamosto's account, it appears that relations between the
Portuguese and the native peoples in this part of the coast were very
cordial. Budomel saw to it that Cadamosto was royally entertained
and invited his guest to enter the local mosque where he himself worshiped. Also, as it was now common practice for Henry's mariners
to be accompanied by African slaves who spoke Portuguese, the African chief and the Venetian sea trader were able to talk about the
Christian faith. From what Budomel said, Cadamosto was certain
that only the fear of losing power among his own people prevented
the chief from converting to Christianity.

The most distant point reached by Cadamosto on this, his first voyage for Prince Henry, was the mouth of the Gambia River. This river
ran 100 miles south of Cape Verde, in present-day Gambia. But, although
he had made no notable discoveries, he had taken careful note of all he
had seen. Years later, when he wrote an account of his travels, he recalled
vividly his first sight of lions, elephants, and hippopotamuses, his first
taste of ostrich eggs, and his first observations in the unfamiliar skies
over Africa of constellations he had never seen before.

Above: the Senegal River. Known then
as Senega, the mouth was entered by
Dinis Dias in 1445. He thought it was
the western arm of the Nile.

Left: trading has probably not changed
very substantially in the last 500
years and the goods that the
Portuguese brought back were
probably acquired in markets not
very different from this one at
Abidjan on the Ivory Coast of
West Africa. Built on a peninsula into
a lagoon, Abidjan has become one of
the best ports in West Africa.

Right: traditional designs of silverware
made by Kabyle craftsmen from
Algeria and northwestern Tunisia.
These examples show a pendant,
bracelets, a pair of brooches, and a
trinket box of the type that would
have been fashionable in the 1500's.

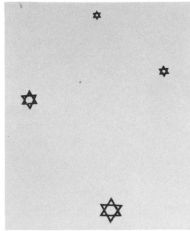

Left: the Southern Cross (Crux Australis) was probably the constellation that Cadamosto described in the account of his journeys. It is in the path of the Milky Way and its bright stars form a small, but well-defined cross, the upright of which points almost to the south celestial pole. The constellation was an entirely new one to the first Portuguese explorers, since it is not visible much north of the Equator.

Within a year of his return to Portugal, Cadamosto set out again, this time with three caravels. Leaving Lagos in early May, he sailed past the Canaries without stopping, and made straight for Cape Blanc. Just off that cape, he tells us, his ships were overtaken by a fierce storm which carried them off course in a southwesterly direction for several days. In this way, Cadamosto says, his ships came upon two large undiscovered islands—part of a large group off Cape Verde. The truth of Cadamosto's claim that he himself was the original discoverer of the islands is doubtful.

When the storm that had driven him off course subsided, Cadamosto again followed the coast southward. He first revisited the area around the Senegal River, and then sailed on to the mouth of the Gambia River.

Above: hippopotamuses on the banks of a river in Africa. These animals are extremely large and ungainly, with thick bodies and short legs, but they are surprisingly agile. Their hairless skin is almost two inches thick in places. They spend much of their time in water and their eyes and nostrils protrude to enable the animal to see and breathe while floating. The exotic animals of Africa were a source of wonder to the explorers, who continually commented upon them in the records of their voyages.

Below: an African woman selling beads in the market at Cotonou, Dahomey, in West Africa. Once used as a currency for buying slaves, beads have always been, and in fact still are, an important article of trade all over the African continent.

After traveling many miles up the river (along whose banks he saw numerous elephants and hippopotamuses), he encountered a native tribe. With the chief of this tribe, one Batti-Mansa, he traded some of his European goods for slaves and a little gold. In addition, Cadamosto was given many presents, including gold ornaments, fruit, and exotic animals. He then traveled some 100 miles farther south along the coast to the Bissagos Islands (opposite present-day Portuguese Guinea). But, finding trade impossible because none of his interpreters could speak the local language, he set sail for home.

In 1458 — that is about two years after Cadamosto had made his second voyage — another expedition was also engaged in exploring and trading along the African coastline. It consisted of three caravels under the command of Diogo Gomes, a man of Prince Henry's household. Apparently Gomes' vessels followed much the same course as Cadamosto's. Like Cadamosto, Gomes sailed up the Gambia River, where he too did some trading. He seems to have done rather better in this regard than Cadamosto, however, for he succeeded in obtaining some 180 pounds of gold for the cloth and beads he had brought with him. Existing accounts tell us little more about his expedition, apart from noting that Gomes was the first Portuguese navigator to use the quadrant.

By the time that Cadamosto and Gomes returned home, Henry was nearing 70 and far from well. He died in November, 1460, never having seen the distant lands to whose shores he had sent so many mariners. Yet, through the reports of his captains and correspondents, and through his careful study of all the known facts about West Africa, he had come to know more about this part of the world than any other man of his time.

For 40 years, Henry the Navigator had persevered, with infinite patience and unshakable determination, in forwarding the cause of Portuguese exploration. He, and he alone, had provided the initiative, guidance, and financial backing for this first history-making period of Portuguese exploration. Who would now take up his vital role as exploration's sponsor and director?

Henry's lifelong generosity to his pilots, together with his willingness to bear the loss of commercially unsuccessful voyages, had so impoverished him that he had died heavily in debt. Neither King Alfonso V nor his brother, Fernando, who was legally Henry's heir, wished to be placed in a similar financial position. What is more, both brothers were far more interested in crusading against the Moslems in

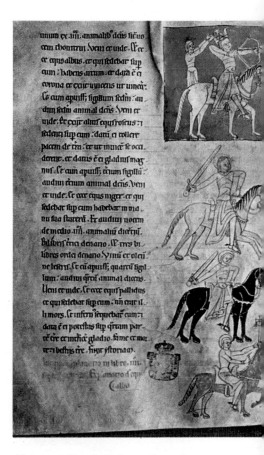

Above: an illuminated page from the Comentario do Apocalipse de Lorvao, showing Portuguese horsemen preparing for a crusade against the Moors at the time of Alfonso Henriques (1112—1185).

69

Right: the voyages which rounded the hump of Africa, eventually moving down across the Gulf of Guinea to the south.

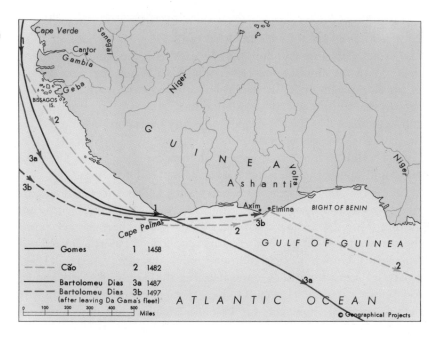

Below: old fort at Dahomey on the Slave Coast of West Africa. The part of the coast fronting onto the Bight of Benin, which includes Dahomey and Lagos, became known as the Slave Coast because, for 300 years, it was the main source of African slaves.

Morocco than in attempting to outflank Islam by exploration.

Nevertheless, Henry's work had made exploration part and parcel of Portugal's way of life. And many strictly business-minded men in the kingdom knew that voyages to Africa would become increasingly profitable in terms of trade. Even King Alfonso, indifferent as he might have been to exploration for its own sake, saw its value in furthering trade. And, indeed, it was to be a hardheaded commercial contract that ultimately opened the way for the next great period of Portuguese exploration.

For the first few years after Henry's death, however, very few ships sailed farther afield than before. Contemporary records speak of only one expedition—that of Pedro de Sintra—that achieved anything significant during these years. In 1462, De Sintra surpassed Alvaro Fernandes' 1446 voyage to Sierra Leone by sailing several hundred miles farther on to the coast of what is now Liberia. Meanwhile, trade with Guinea continued, and Diogo Gomes and other captains completed the exploration of all 10 of the Cape Verde Islands.

Then, in 1469, King Alfonso made a unique, five-year agreement with a wealthy Lisbon citizen named Fernão Gomes. In return for exclusive trading rights along the Guinea coast, and all the profits he

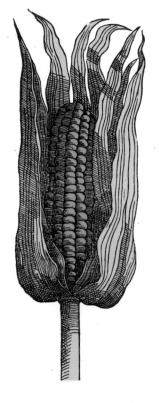

could make from them, Gomes undertook to sponsor the exploration of 400 miles of new coastline every year for five years. This contract, which made it possible for Portuguese exploration to continue at no cost whatsoever to the king, must be one of the most extraordinary in history. Still more extraordinary is the fact that it worked. Gomes did not lose by it, since we know that he grew rich enough to contribute handsomely toward the cost of King Alfonso's crusades in Morocco. And Portuguese exploration certainly gained by it, for in five years the seamen in Gomes' employ explored 2,000 miles of previously unknown African coastline.

Unfortunately, none of Gomes' captains wrote of their adventures as Cadamosto had written of his. Moreover, because exploration was now in private hands, there was no royal historian like Azurara to record their deeds. All that contemporary records tell us of this momentous period of exploration is a few names and a few facts.

We do know that one captain, named Da Costa, sailed beyond Liberia to Axum, on the coast of present-day Ghana. Axum later became a fortified center for Portugal's burgeoning gold trade. Then Pero de Escolar and João de Santarem sailed 100 miles beyond Axum, to Elmina (also on the Ghana coast). These men, in contrast to their pre-

Above: African woman pounding corn and taro root. Both became staple foods for the African peoples. Taro is an herbaceous plant with bulbous underground tubers. It has a very high nutritional value and, when ground down, is mixed into a paste of varying thicknesses.
Above left: an early drawing of mealie corn, described by the Italian geographer, Ramusio, as "the miraculous and famous corn called maize in the India occidental, on which half the world nourishes itself...." Maize was introduced into Europe as a result of the voyages of Christopher Columbus.

Above: John II (1455—1495), known as "the Perfect," succeeded his father, Alfonso V, in 1481. He was already much involved in Portuguese exploration and continued to take an interest as king. It was in his reign that Bartolomeu Dias discovered the Cape of Good Hope.

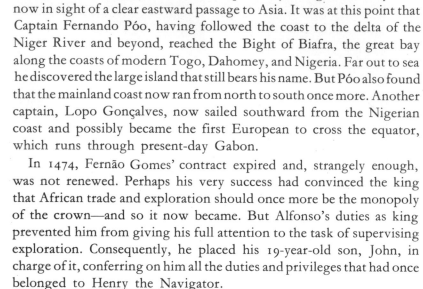

Right: the epic voyages down the coast of Africa searching for the way to the Indies. The brown areas are the vast expanses still unknown to the outside world during the period of the voyages.

Above: the Congo, largest river in Africa, second only to the Amazon in the world. The mouth was discovered by Diogo Cão in 1482 when he erected a marble pillar on what is now called Sharks Point, recording the discovery, and claiming the land for Portugal. At first the river was called Rio do Padroa (pillar river), or Zaire (native word meaning "big water") but it was finally named Congo, after the ancient kingdom called Kongo.

decessors, found themselves following the African coast in an easterly, rather than a southerly direction, and probably thought that they were now in sight of a clear eastward passage to Asia. It was at this point that Captain Fernando Póo, having followed the coast to the delta of the Niger River and beyond, reached the Bight of Biafra, the great bay along the coasts of modern Togo, Dahomey, and Nigeria. Far out to sea he discovered the large island that still bears his name. But Póo also found that the mainland coast now ran from north to south once more. Another captain, Lopo Gonçalves, now sailed southward from the Nigerian coast and possibly became the first European to cross the equator, which runs through present-day Gabon.

In 1474, Fernão Gomes' contract expired and, strangely enough, was not renewed. Perhaps his very success had convinced the king that African trade and exploration should once more be the monopoly of the crown—and so it now became. But Alfonso's duties as king prevented him from giving his full attention to the task of supervising exploration. Consequently, he placed his 19-year-old son, John, in charge of it, conferring on him all the duties and privileges that had once belonged to Henry the Navigator.

John had all of Henry's enthusiasm for exploration, and all his determination to outflank Islam and capture a share of the Far East trade. He was an impatient man, bent on quick results, and was as ready to punish as to reward in his eagerness to achieve his goals. Nevertheless, he was unable to get on with his task for several years. From 1475 to 1479, Portugal was involved in a war with Castile, and John himself served as a soldier. Then, in 1481, his father died, and the whole responsibility for governing the country fell upon his shoulders.

Even so, King John II, as he then became, at once showed his interest in the cause of Portuguese exploration. Almost immediately after his accession to the throne, he ordered the rebuilding of the fortifications at Arguim, and the construction of a new fort at Elmina, on the Ghanaian coast. His orders made it clear that he expected these places to serve not only as trading posts, but also as future springboards for new voyages of discovery. The very next year he sent out Diogo Cão to make the first of those voyages.

That extraordinary marine contractor, Fernão Gomes, had set a record by pushing discovery forward at the rate of 400 miles a year. Now, in a single voyage, Diogo Cão pioneered some 850 miles of unexplored coastline. After leaving Elmina, where he stopped to take on provi-

BLACK SEA

MEDITERRANEAN SEA

RED SEA

TROPIC OF CANCER

Nile

AZORES
TERCEIRA
Lisbon
Lagos
PORTO SANTO
MADEIRAS
STR. OF GIBRALTAR
Ceuta
CANARY ISLANDS
TROPIC OF CANCER
Cape Bojador
Rio de Oro
Cape Blanc
ARGUIM I.
CAPE VERDE ISLANDS
Senegal
Cape Verde
Cantor
Gambia
BISSAGOS IS.
Niger
Cape Palmas
Axim Elmina
BIGHT OF BENIN
B. OF BIAFRA
FERNANDO PÓ
GULF OF GUINEA
PRÍNCIPE
SÃO TOMÉ
ANNOBÓN
Cape St. Catherine
EQUATOR

Congo

Lake Victoria

Lake Tanganyika

Mouth of the Congo

ATLANTIC

OCEAN

ASCENSION I.

ST. HELENA

Cape St. Mary
(Cape Lobo)
MONTE NEGRO

Lake Malawi

Zambesi

Sofala

Cape Cross
WALVIS BAY

TROPIC OF CAPRICORN

TROPIC OF CAPRICORN
Cape Corrientes

Cabo da Volta
(Dias Pt.)

Orange

Natal

ST. HELENA BAY

MOSSEL BAY

ALGOA BAY

Cape of Good Hope

INDIAN

OCEAN

Gonçalo Cabral	1	1432
Eannes	2a	1433
	2b	1433
	2c	1435
Baldaya	3	1436
Da Cadamosto	4a	1455
	4b	1456
Gomes	5	1458-60
Cão	6a	1482
	6b	1485
Bartolomeu Dias	7	1487
Da Gama	8	1497-9
(B. Dias after leaving Da Gama 8A)		
Pedro Cabral	9	1500
(with Diogo Dias 9A)		

0 200 400 600 800 1000
Miles

TRISTAN DE CUNHA

© Geographical Project

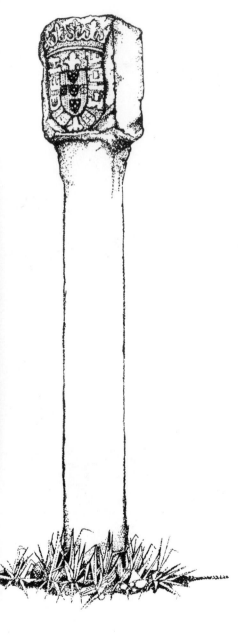

Above: drawing from a book by Diogo Cão which was published in Lisbon. It shows the "Padroa de Santo Agostinho," the pillar, bearing the arms of Portugal, which Cão erected at Cape St. Mary, or as it was then known, "Santo Agostinho."

sions, he pressed on to Cape St. Catherine, just south of the equator. St. Catherine marked the very farthest limits of Portuguese navigation so far reached. After three landings made in search of drinking water, Cão came to an area where the ocean water itself was almost as fresh as waters of a lake. This could only mean that he was near the mouth of a mighty river. Sailing shoreward, Cão soon found himself between the banks of the great Congo River. Some way up the river he sighted a village, and, although none of his own interpreters could speak the inhabitants' language, he conversed with them by means of signs, and even managed to trade with them. Then, having set up on the south bank of the river a great stone pillar bearing the arms of Portugal, he continued southward along the coast. He erected a second pillar at Cape St. Mary, more than half the way down the coast of present-day Angola, before he returned home in the early spring of 1484.

King John II was delighted—as well he might have been—with the success of Cão's voyage. The king rewarded Cão generously, and then sent him off again to attempt an even longer voyage.

Little is known about Cão's second voyage. It may have begun in 1484 or in 1485; Cão himself may have arrived home again safely or he may have died on the return journey. On these points contemporary accounts differ. Nevertheless, it is certain that Cão far excelled his first effort, for he again erected two commemorative pillars. The first was put up on the high headland of Cape Negro, more than 100 miles farther south than Cape St. Mary; the second was erected at Cape Cross, less than 200 miles from the Tropic of Capricorn, in present-day South West Africa.

Ptolemy, the master geographer and astronomer of antiquity, had maintained that a huge bridge of land joined southern Africa to southeast Asia, making of the Indian Ocean an enormous land-locked sea. Portugal's hope of pioneering a sea route to East Asia rested on the optimistic premise that Ptolemy was wrong, and that beyond the southern limits of Africa, the Atlantic Ocean merged with the Indian Ocean.

King John felt that Cão must surely have come within reach of Africa's southernmost point, and he was impatient to put the matter to the test. Adding to his burning interest in this question was the fact that, in 1486, he had learned (from a Portuguese trader who lived in Benin) of the existence of a powerful Christian king named Ogané who ruled in East Africa. This king, John thought, might well be the legendary Prester John or one of his descendants. John believed that if Portu-

guese seamen could pass beyond southern Africa and into the Indian
Ocean, they might accomplish two very important things in one stroke.
Not only might they secure for Portugal a share in the lucrative spice
trade with the East; they might also make the long hoped-for alliance
with Prester John's kingdom and presumably powerful resources.

To make a start toward accomplishing this dual aim, King John now
dispatched an expedition under the command of one Bartolomeu
Dias. His mission was to travel southward along the coast of Africa
until he reached the southernmost tip of Africa, and then to sail northeast into the Indian Ocean.

Dias set out from Lisbon in August, 1487, with two small caravels
and a slower, broader-beamed store ship to carry extra food supplies.
Among the items the fleet carried with them were three commemorative stone pillars. Not one was to be erected until the expedition had
passed Diogo Cão's last landing point.

As far as Cape Cross, Dias probably followed much the same course
as Cão had taken. Not far beyond it, and now in unknown waters, he
came to Walvis Bay (halfway down the coast of present day South West
Africa) and there, it seems, he left his cumbersome supply ship. Then
he sailed on for some 400 miles. Not until he reached a point close to
the mouth of the Orange River (now the boundary between South
West Africa and South Africa), did he erect his first pillar. After a few
more days at sea, his ships were caught in a fierce storm, and were driven
steadily southward, out of sight of land, for nearly two weeks.

Above: Benin sculpture in bronze of a
warrior-horseman. Negro sculpture
from Benin and other parts of Africa,
has had an increasing influence
on sculpture in other parts of the world.

75

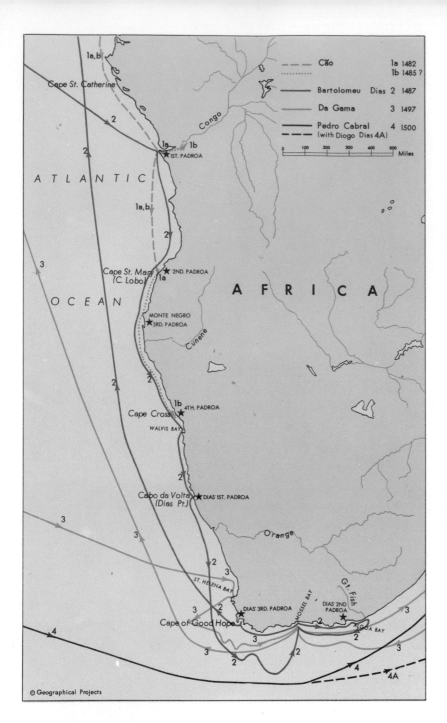

Above: the final stages of exploration down around the Cape of Good Hope.

When the storm abated, Dias naturally sailed eastward, as Portuguese sailors had done for the past 70 years when, in sailing along the African coast, they had wished to put in to land. Yet, after several days of sailing east, Dias saw no sight of land. Then, beginning to suspect the truth, he turned northward, and soon afterward reached what is now called Mossel Bay. He was halfway along Africa's southern coast.

Realizing that he had, in fact, found the southern limits of the great continent, Dias now traveled farther east, and set up a second stone pillar near Algoa Bay, close to the point at which the south coast of Africa begins curving northward. By now, however, his crew believed

themselves to be dangerously far from their store ship, and insisted on turning back. On the return journey, they came to a great cape which—because of the storm that had prevented him from seeing it on the outward voyage — Dias named the Cape of Storms. There he erected his third and last pillar before making sail for Portugal.

In December, 1488, when Dias returned, John II received his report with relief and joy. But he did not approve of Dias' name for the great cape. John knew that this cape, which marked the southern extremity of Africa, held out the promise of a clear sea route to the Indies. For this reason he renamed it the Cape of Good Hope.

Above: the Cape of Good Hope, so named by King John II of Portugal after its discovery by Bartolomeu Dias. Dias, who was blown round it in a gale, had called it Cabo Tormentoso (Capo of Stormo), but King John thought his name more appropriate for the promontory marking the southernmost extremity of Africa, discovery of which had opened up an ocean route to the Indies.

Below: this sort of opulent picture of the East—here, the birthday party of the Kublai Khan from a manuscript of the travels of Marco Polo—presented an alluring prospect of riches for the country and men able to bypass the Arab middlemen. Bodleian Library MS. Bodley 264, fol. 239.

West to Revelation
5

For a number of years prior to Bartolomeu Dias' voyage, King John had been pestered by a strange young man who claimed to know a sea route to the Indies. In 1484, John had called a committee of experts to assess this plan. The committee finally dismissed it as impossible, and the young man, thoroughly discouraged, had left the country. The young man's name was Christopher Columbus.

Several months after Dias had left for Africa, however, King John had begun to have second thoughts about Christopher Columbus' idea, and had made it known that he would welcome him back. But Columbus did not choose to come back, and John was forced to content himself with the hope that Dias would be successful. The king was still not at all sure that the Indies could be reached by rounding southern Africa, and he feared that, by dismissing Columbus, he had also thrown away the only clue to a possible alternative route. He was vastly relieved, therefore, to hear Dias' promising report on his return from the Cape of Good Hope. Now, perhaps, John could forget the fanciful theories of young Columbus. Little did he know that one day those same fanciful theories would result in one of the world's most historic voyages.

Not much is known about the early life of the man who, at successive stages, styled himself Colombo, Colom, Colomo, and Colon, except that he almost certainly was born in Genoa in 1451, and was the son of a weaver. We also know that he had two brothers, one of whom, Bartholomew, became a highly skilled mapmaker. Columbus himself took to the sea at an early age to make what money he could by trading.

During his early years at sea, Columbus learned a great deal, not only about navigation. He was of a studious nature, and the slow sea passages of those days gave him time to read whatever came to hand. Although he had little formal education, he soon became proficient in Latin, and very knowledgeable about the cosmographical theories then prevalent in Europe. He also got to know the scriptures thoroughly, particularly the books of prophecy. It may have been this that gradually convinced the young seaman that God had destined him to perform great deeds—deeds connected with the sea.

In 1476, he sailed with a French corsair fleet which attacked some Italian ships off the tip of Portugal. In the ensuing battle Columbus' vessel caught fire, and, preferring immersion to incineration, he jumped overboard and struck out for land. The swim was a long one, but at last, completely exhausted, he found the solid ground of Portugal beneath his feet.

Columbus regarded the strange turn of events that had brought him to Portugal as a sign from God. Although a man of strong family feeling, he had never felt any sense of loyalty to his native city of Genoa. If God had now seen fit to cast him up on Portuguese shores, then he would look to Portugal for help in furthering his life's work. He could hardly have come to a more appropriate place than this land of explorers.

He quickly seized whatever opportunities for ocean travel Portugal could offer. Within a year of his arrival, as he himself wrote later, he had visited Thule (by which he meant Iceland) and sailed 100 leagues beyond it. This journey must have meant much to him as the first step in realizing his destiny, for we know that he had already translated the following prophetic passage from Seneca's *Medea*: "There will come a time when a great part of the earth will be opened up, and a new sailor... shall discover a new world, and Thule shall no longer be the last of lands."

Perhaps, too, while sailing the silent opal seas of the Arctic, Columbus heard tales of the ancient Vikings, who had voyaged westward to Greenland, and thence southwest to a land called Vinland. Whether or not such tales could be authenticated, Columbus would have believed them, for he was firmly convinced that there *were* lands that could be reached by sailing across the Atlantic. The fact that in the Viking

Right: details of the birth and early life of Christopher Columbus are uncertain, but he was probably born in Genoa in 1451. What is certain, however, is that at a very early age he became a sailor and that he made many voyages with the Portuguese fleet, after being shipwrecked off Lisbon in 1476. During his voyages, and because of his reading, he became convinced that it would be possible to reach Asia by sailing west.

sagas they were called "Vinland" was of no importance; he was certain that they were none other than the lands of eastern Asia.

During the next few years, he took part in various Portuguese voyages to Porto Santo, Madeira, and the Guinea coast. From the men he met, he picked up more hints of lands across the Atlantic. Among other things, he learned the curious fact that, on the coasts of Madeira, the Canaries, and the Azores, carved wooden statuettes were occasionally washed ashore when the wind blew strongly and steadily from the west. Once, he was told, the seas running before a strong west wind had even washed up the body of a man whose features were neither European nor of any known African race.

Above: this Catalan map of 1375 was the sort of map available to Henry the Navigator and his scholars. The areas which were well-known were correctly charted, but outside the well-traversed ways the picture was very sketchy.

81

Other men had heard these tales with relative indifference. Maybe there *were* distant lands to the west, but what of it? Portuguese seamen had already found the Cape Verde Islands and the Azores. Possibly there were other islands still farther away. But to make a deliberate search for them would be as hopeless as looking for a needle in a haystack. Columbus, however, heard these tales with avid interest, for they offered substantiation for his own developing geographical theories.

Ironically, these theories—which were ultimately to lead Columbus to the New World—were based on a mass of misinformation and erroneous conclusions. He had read in the Apocrypha that "Upon the third day Thou didst command that the waters should be gathered in the seventh part of the earth: six parts hast Thou dried up...." On the basis of this text, he had concluded that six-sevenths of the globe was made up of dry land, the seventh of water.

Like most well-read men of this time, Columbus accepted the fact that the earth is round, and it seemed quite logical to him that the combined landmasses of Europe, Africa, and Asia should occupy the requi-

Above: waterfall at Gullfoss ("golden waterfall") in southwest Iceland. Waterfalls are a common sight on this island in the North Atlantic, the most northerly point of which is on the Arctic circle. Columbus claimed to have visited Iceland in the late 1400's. For many years it was considered the last land of the world.

Left: Genoa, port of Liguria, Italy, from the Nuremburg Chronicles of 1493. The prowess of Genoese sailors against the Saracens led to the growth of a powerful navy and it is therefore not surprising that, being born into such an atmosphere, Columbus chose a maritime career.

site six-sevenths of the globe. If all the oceans together occupied the remaining seventh, the Atlantic could not be so very large after all! Indeed, from his study of the writings of Ptolemy and Marco Polo, he had concluded that the land between West Africa and eastern Asia stretched eastward through more than 280° out of the total 360° comprising the earth's circumference. Thus, he reasoned, the distance *westward* from West Africa to eastern Asia could be traversed by voyaging through less than 80° of longitude.

It remained only to translate that figure into miles. Here Columbus made still another error. Unaware that the Arab mile is longer than the European, he used the Arab figure of $62\frac{1}{2}$ miles per degree of longitude at the equator. (There are actually 69 European miles per degree of longitude at the equator). Then, deciding that the first transatlantic voyage could best be made in the latitude of the Canaries, where a degree of longitude is smaller than at the equator, he whittled the figure still further down to 50 miles per degree of longitude. Multiplying 50 miles by 80° of longitude, he then came up with the figure of 4,000

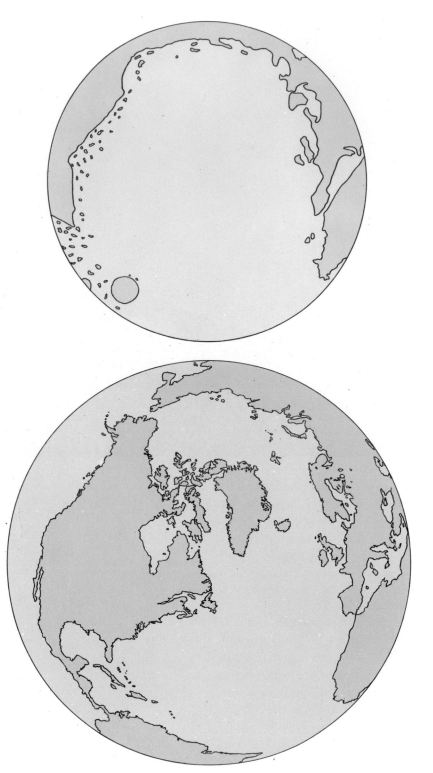

Left: the upper globe shows the world as Columbus must have imagined it from his inaccurate calculations. The lower globe shows the actual proportions, with the unsuspected New World squarely in the path from Europe to the Asian coast.

miles as a measurement of the distance from the Canaries to eastern Asia.

Columbus was somewhat vague about his ultimate destination, since he, like most other men in the Europe of 1492, had only a rough idea of Far Eastern geography. He therefore described his goal variously as Cathay (China), Cipango (Japan), India, the Indies, or the Empire of the Great Khan. Nevertheless, he knew roughly what he meant, and so did everyone he talked to about his great plan.

The man he most wanted to talk to, of course, was "the perfect king," John II of Portugal. How did Columbus, a foreigner of humble origin, gain an audience with the king? It happened (perhaps not entirely by accident) that whenever he was in Lisbon he chose to worship at a convent which was also a home for daughters of the nobility. Columbus was tall, red-haired, handsome, and not without charm. Before long, one of the high-born ladies at the convent had succumbed to his attractions and married him. Marriage into a noble family, of course, made it only a matter of time before Columbus gained access to the royal family.

The young seaman began trying to persuade John of his theories in 1478 (three years before John became king), and kept on trying for four fruitless years. It is not known in precisely what way he unfolded his ideas, but, since he was both secretive and given to exaggeration, it is reasonable to suppose that he presented them with certain significant omissions and fanciful additions. He doubtless left out what he believed to be the main points of evidence for the new sea route, fearing that others might profit from the information and rob him of the glory of discovery. And, in order to gain John's support, he no doubt elaborated on the fabulous wealth of the Orient and stressed the ease with which Portugal might obtain it using his route.

King John, however, was not convinced by Columbus' presentation. Moreover, he was aghast at the high value which this upstart seaman placed on his services. Columbus was demanding nothing less than a knighthood, the title of admiral, the viceroyalty of all the lands he might discover, and a tenth of the value of "all profitable things" found in them. Nevertheless, John did not dismiss the scheme entirely until 1482, when a council of learned men pronounced it impossible.

Disappointed in Portugal, Columbus decided to offer his plan to other monarchs. In 1485, already widowed and with a small son to provide for, he went to Spain, the recently united kingdom of King Ferdinand of Aragon and Queen Isabella of Castile.

Below: it must have been such books that Columbus studied while seeking royal support in Portugal and Spain.

Above: view of Lisbon from the Castello de São Jorge, showing typical terraced houses built into the surrounding hills. The city is divided into five districts and the Castle of St. George is a notable feature of one of them, Lisboa Oriental. Once a Moorish citadel, it was later converted into a fort and barracks. Columbus met his wife, daughter of a noble family, at a convent in Lisbon, giving him his desired entrée to the court.

In Spain, Columbus found his first friends among the learned monks and wealthy seamen of the port of Palos. They were impressed by his strange visionary scheme, and introduced him to certain noblemen who had access to the king and queen. In this way, Columbus gained his second chance to present his theories before royalty. Again he unfolded his great plan—mysteriously, guardedly, and with embellishments; again he demanded the same exorbitant price for his services; and again he persevered for six years without success. Indeed, in 1488, he thought seriously of going back to King John, but although the Portuguese king expressed himself willing to see Columbus, he did not go. Probably he refrained from doing so because at this time his brother Bartholomew was—unsuccessfully—laying the plan before England's King Henry VII.

In 1492, however, Columbus' long battle for royal support met with

sudden success. In January of that year, Ferdinand and Isabella's forces captured the city of Granada, the last Moorish stronghold on Spanish soil. Euphoric over this victory, they generously decided to sponsor Columbus' scheme and ensure that he had ships, men, and supplies. They even accepted his outrageous terms with scarcely a reservation.

By the beginning of August, 1492, three caravels, under the command of Admiral Christobal Colon (as he now called himself), lay ready in the harbor at Palos. His flagship, of which he was also captain, was the *Santa María*. It was about 115 feet long, with a deck length of over 60 feet. Her three masts, unlike those of most caravels, carried square sails. The *Pinta*, faster, but less than half the length of the flagship, was similarly rigged. The third ship, the *Niña*, was even smaller than the *Pinta*, and was conventionally lateen-rigged.

Although the ships sailed in those days were small, Columbus thought

Above: the refectory of the Franciscan monastery of La Rábida, Palos, where the despairing Columbus went in 1485 when yet another attempt to enlist aid for his venture had failed. It was through Juan Perez, of the monastery, that Queen Isabella finally agreed to his terms and it was from Palos that he sailed on August 3, 1492.

them quite big enough to undertake the voyage across the Atlantic. In fact, for later voyages of discovery, he came to prefer vessels as small as the *Niña* to those as big as the *Santa María*.

Columbus was well pleased with his captains as well. Both Martin Pinzón, captain of the *Pinta,* and his brother Vincente, captain of the *Niña*, were experienced mariners. The brothers had also supplied much of the financial backing for the voyage, and could be depended on to do their utmost to ensure its success.

As to the sailors on board the three vessels, Columbus seems to have been confident that he had with him a sufficient number of "good and seasoned seamen." They were, however, a motley crew. Some 20 or 30 of the men were friends of Columbus, domestic servants, or officers of the king "who fancied to sail out of curiosity." The remaining 90 or so were sailors, shipboys, and pilots. About one fourth of their number were one-time convicts who had been granted pardon in return for their services on this voyage. The others were free men who had been persuaded to take part in the voyage by Martin Pinzón's promises of fame, riches, and the sight of "gold-roofed houses" across the ocean.

At daybreak on the morning of Friday, August 3, 1492, Columbus gave the signal to begin, and the little fleet put out to sea, every sail bellying in the wind. Each ship carried cannon and was stocked with about a six-months' supply of provisions. On board, too, were "slight wares fit for commerce with barbarous people." (Columbus apparently expected to come upon uncivilized off-shore islands before he reached the cultured and luxurious Orient.)

The fleet's short passage to the Canaries should have been routine and uneventful, but it was not. On the way, the *Pinta* twice broke her helm, causing irritating delays. Then there were three days of dead calm, during which all three ships had to lie motionless. When the fleet did reach port, it was kept waiting for a month while the necessary repairs to the *Pinta* were made. Columbus, feverish with impatience, was comforted only by the fact that the enforced delay had provided an opportunity for exchanging the *Niña's* lateen sails for square ones which would increase her speed.

Not until Thursday, September 6, was the fleet able to leave the Canaries and begin its task of sailing westward into the vast uncharted seas of the Atlantic. Ferro, most westerly of the Canary Islands, gave the sailors what many of them already feared might be their last sight of land. Unlike Columbus, they were not at all sure that their voyage would

Above: Ferdinand and Isabella became patrons of Spanish exploration. Here they are seen waving goodbye to an expedition setting off to the Indies.

Left: Palos harbor in southwest Spain, 70 miles from Seville on the estuary of the river Tinto. From this port Columbus sailed on his voyage of discovery to the New World. Inaccessible today to large ships, in Columbus' time it was a busy shipping center.

end in success. Their concern was not surprising because, although most of them were familiar with the methods of navigating by sun, stars, and compass, few of them had ever done so for long out of sight of land. Now, with wholly unknown seas ahead, they had nothing but these ways of finding their way out and back home.

Columbus alone was firm in his belief that the voyage would bring them safely to their destination. His faith in his plan was unshakable; so was his confidence in his own powers; so, as a result, was his courage.

The fleet was sailing along latitude 28° N. Columbus had chosen this course after concluding, from a passage in Marco Polo's book, that in this latitude he would find Cipango (Japan), the great island that lay some 1,500 miles off the coast of Cathay (the traditional name for China). So Columbus and the Pinzóns kept firmly to that course. It proved to be a lucky choice, for it kept the fleet within the belt of favorable trade winds.

As the familiar shores of Europe dropped ever farther behind them, more and more of the sailors on board the three vessels became dubious and fearful. To keep them from panicking, Columbus gave the order that the fleet was to sail nonstop, day and night, for 700 leagues. After that, it was to sail only during daylight hours. He made no promises, but left the crew to draw the obvious conclusions. They did, and took heart. Their admiral clearly did not expect to sight land for 700 leagues, but after that, he was so sure of sighting it that he would risk no night sailing for fear of missing it.

Columbus calculated rightly that this order would keep his crew from worrying for many days. But what then? It was all very well to assure them that they would sight land after 700 leagues, but what if they did not? After all, Cipango was probably a good 1,000 leagues from the Canaries, and, although Columbus hoped to find islands in between, he could not be sure that his hopes would be rewarded. What would happen if there was no land sighted after 700 leagues? There was a frightening possibility the crew might mutiny. To forestall this, Columbus took to keeping two logbooks. One, meant for his eyes alone, recorded the actual distance covered by the fleet each day. The other, which he made available to the crew, gave a shortened version of the distance covered. It was Columbus' fervent hope that, .using this second log, his men might still be waiting to complete the first 700 leagues when they had actually traveled 800 or more.

Meanwhile, another cause for anxiety had presented itself. Along

Above: a model of the *Santa Maria*.
It seems incredible now that anyone
would be bold enough to attempt—
let alone succeed in—crossing the
then-uncharted part of the Atlantic
Ocean in a vessel such as this, a
half-decked ship of 100 tons, with a
crew of only 40 men. Columbus had
faith in himself and in his ship—a
faith which was entirely justified.

Right: early voyages crossing the Atlantic Ocean. The green edges of the American continents show the areas discovered by Europeans by about 1526.

Above: Columbus made entries in his journal after leaving Palos and is thought to have drawn sketches of the ships in his fleet. A book (belonging to Columbus' son, Ferdinand) in the Columbine library in Seville shows a map decorated with the outlines of three such ships.

Below: wooden traverse and wind rose used in conjunction with an hourglass to record changes in direction and speed during watches.

the Atlantic coast of Europe the compass needle always pointed slightly east of north. But a mere four days after Ferro had disappeared from view, Columbus had begun to find that the compass needle was pointing considerably *west* of north. If ever mariners had needed to trust the compass it was here, in mid-ocean. Now, without warning, it was proving inaccurate. The then-unknown problem of the earth's magnetic variation could not have made itself felt at a worse possible moment.

Columbus must have been badly shaken by the discovery that he could not trust his compass, and we can be sure that, from then on, he relied heavily on the Pole Star for direction-finding. But the failure of the compass offered yet another possible cause for alarm among the crew. Columbus knew well how disastrous it would be for their morale to lose faith in the instrument. He therefore let it be known that the trouble lay not in the compass, but in some fault on the part of the Pole Star. This sounded reasonable because it was at that time believed (even by Columbus himself) that the compass needle was attracted by the Pole Star.

However dubious Columbus' methods may seem to us now, they were the only means at his command for calming his crew. By the time they had reached the seaweed-covered waters of the vast Sargasso Sea in the western Atlantic, fear and despair had fixed their grip on almost every man. The king's officers who had come along "out of curiosity" were devoutly wishing themselves back at court; the convicts were longing for the security of their jails; and the honest seamen were yearning for the humdrum routine of sea trading in coastal waters.

To boost their flagging spirits, Columbus told them to look closely at the tangled weeds floating all around them. Were they not, he asked, "very like green grass... recently drifted away from land?" The Pinzóns were quick to add encouraging words of their own. It was they in fact, who, some time later, drew attention to the significance of flights of birds and "showers without wind." Both phenomena, they pointed out, were sure signs that land could not be far off.

On the evening of September 25, Martin Pinzón shouted from the

——	Columbus 1 1492–3 (with the Pinzón brothers)	— · · — · ·	Vespucci 8 1501–
— — —	Columbus 2 1493–6	— · — · —	Pedro Cabral 9 1500
— · — · —	Columbus 3 1498	——	Gaspar Corte-Real 10 1500
· · · · · ·	Columbus 4 1502–3	— — —	Gaspar Corte-Real 11 1501 (with Miguel Corte-Real 11A)
——	John Cabot 5 1497 (with young Sebastian Cabot)	· · · · · ·	Miguel Corte-Real 12 1502
· · · · · ·	John Cabot 6 1498	— · · — · ·	Sebastian Cabot 13 1509
— · — · —	Vespucci 7 1499–1500	— — —	Sebastian Cabot 14 1526

Miles Equatorial Scale

Geographical Projects

Right: the beach at San Salvador where Columbus landed on October 12, 1492. This island in the Bahamas, known as Guanahani to the native peoples inhabiting it, was renamed San Salvador by Columbus and his arrival marked the discovery of the New World.

Above: frigate bird, a large sea bird, one species of which is found in the Atlantic. They have extremely long, slender wings, a forked tail, and a long, hooked beak, with which they attack and rob other sea birds. Frigates do not alight on water, as they have no oil glands to waterproof their feathers, but they are extremely skillful in the air and dive to catch fish dropped by the birds they attack. Birds such as this have always been well-known to sailors as a sign they are nearing land.

castle of the *Pinta* that he had sighted land. The fleet changed course immediately, and headed in the direction of the sighting. But the light of the following sunrise revealed only an unbroken horizon of sea and sky. The crew's disappointment quickly turned to anger at their commander, and some began to talk of mutiny. The Pinzóns, when they heard of this, were strongly in favor of hanging the ringleaders. Columbus, however, was willing to overlook the conspirators' treachery, provided they would agree to sail on for a few more days. Realizing that they would find no mercy at the hands of the Pinzóns if they did rebel against Columbus, the would-be mutineers accepted his offer and the fleet sailed on.

On October 7, wisely taking his clue from the direction of a flight of birds, the admiral changed to a southwesterly course. Several days later, sticks and reeds were seen floating by. Land could not be far off now! On the night of October 11, just before 12 P. M., Columbus thought he saw the light of a fire shining dimly in the distance. But only one other man on board the *Santa María* agreed with him. Then early the next morning a cannon shot—the prearranged signal for a positive sighting of land—boomed out from the *Pinta's* bows.

This must have been Columbus' supreme moment. At long last his efforts had been rewarded and his dream fulfilled; he had reached Asia by sailing west. He did not know—and would never know—that a continent and another ocean still separated him from the Orient.

When land was sighted, the fleet was lying off the coast of Guanahani (later called San Salvador) in the Bahamas, some 500 miles southeast of Florida. On the morning of October 12, the Admiral of the Ocean Sea went ashore, and formally took possession of the island for Ferdinand and Isabella. These proceedings were regarded with curiosity

by the island's copper-skinned inhabitants, who had gathered to watch the white man's arrival. Columbus soon made friends with them and did some trading, exchanging various "slight wares" for parrots and little ornaments of gold.

For the next few days, Columbus explored this island and others in the Bahamas. He sought in vain for the source of the gold from which the islanders' ornaments were made, but did ascertain that the island possessed many other valuable raw materials: oak, pine, and what he thought to be cinnamon and musk.

The natives had given him to understand that there was another very large island (Cuba) to the southwest. And so, on October 23, after writing in his journal that "it must be Cipango, according to what these people tell me of its size and wealth," he set out to find it. With him he took seven Guanahani islanders.

Inside a week he had reached Cuba and begun to explore it. Its northern coast was so long that he decided that this was not, after all, the island of Cipango, but rather the edge of the Asian mainland itself. Perhaps, even now, he was at the outer limits of the Great Khan's empire. He and his men were charmed by the country's beauty and by its gentle, tobacco-smoking men and women. But Columbus was anxious to move on. If this were indeed the mainland of Cathay, then Cipango could not be far off, and he wanted to find it. Martin Pinzón seems to have had the same object in mind, for one November day, while the fleet was busy charting Cuba's north coast, he and his crew slipped away in the *Pinta*.

Columbus, left with only the *Santa María* and the *Niña*, was prevented from leaving the shores of Cuba for some time by contrary winds. Early in December, however, he managed to reach Haiti, the great

Above: illustration from the first edition in 1493 of Columbus' letter reporting his discovery. It shows the Spanish idea of American Indians. Observe the ship has oars, which of course none of Columbus' ships had.

Above: an aerial view of Haiti, an island in the West Indies to which Columbus gave the name La Española (later corrupted to Hispaniola), when he discovered it in the early 1490's. He found an island inhabited by Indians who were obviously competent farmers and fishermen, for the island was well cultivated.

island southwest of San Salvador. This island, which he found even more pleasing than Cuba, must certainly be Cipango, for here gold was to be found in great quantity. Certainly the Haitian natives were not at all hesitant about exchanging the precious metal for the "slight wares" Columbus had brought with him.

During his stay in Haiti, Columbus noted with delight the island's cultivated valleys, stands of valuable timber, and splendid climate. As a compliment to the European kingdom that had sponsored his voyage, he named the island La Española (later called Hispaniola).

But the island did not prove lucky for Columbus. On Christmas Eve, disaster befell the *Santa María* as she lay at anchor on the coast. Every man on board was asleep save for a boy whose duty it was to keep watch. It was an exceptionally calm night and there seemed no reason to have a more experienced man at the helm. This reasoning proved fatal for the ship, however, for somehow she ran aground and was so badly damaged that she could never be refloated.

Columbus was now left with two crews and only one ship. Bowing before what he took to be God's will, he decided to leave some 40 of his men on the island as settlers. He and the rest of the crew would sail back to Spain in the *Niña* to report the success of the voyage.

On January 16, 1493, when Columbus set sail for home, he had no qualms about the welfare of the men he had left behind. The island was fruitful, and the Haitian natives had shown themselves to be friendly and cooperative. Alas, when he returned to Haiti on his second voyage the following year, he was to find to his horror that every single one of his men had been killed by the islanders.

On January 18, 1493, two days after Columbus had set off for Spain, he met up with the *Pinta*. He had a short, sharp quarrel with the truant Martin Pinzón, and then gave the order that the two ships were to sail on together. The eastward passage was made in a more northerly latitude than the outward voyage, and in the trip's later stages the two vessels encountered far worse weather. Both caravels were taking in a great deal of water, and when a storm hit them in February there was scarcely a man on board who did not fear for his life. It seemed a miracle, therefore, when, on February 18, they sighted Santa Maria, the southernmost island of the Azores. Here the two vessels anchored, and Columbus gave his men permission to go ashore, find a church, and offer thanks for their deliverance.

The Portuguese governor of the island, however, did not take kindly to the idea of Spanish ships in Portuguese waters. He ordered the would-be worshipers seized and had them imprisoned. The men were released only after several days of negotiation, during which Columbus had to show the governor the documents from Ferdinand and Isabella which proved him to be an admiral and a viceroy.

A fierce storm was now brewing. But, after the governor's inhospitable treatment of his men, Columbus thought it well to get away quickly, whatever the weather. The storm winds were so strong that, even with bare masts, the caravels were driven eastward with perilous swiftness for several days. During this time, the two ships became separated. (Columbus did not see Martin Pinzón again until two weeks later, when, within hours of each other the *Niña* and *Pinta* arrived back in Palos.)

On March 4, the *Niña* reached the mouth of the Tagus River on the coast of Portugal. Here the Spanish ship was approached by an armed Portuguese vessel whose captain boarded the *Niña* and demanded that Columbus explain his presence in Portuguese waters. The proud admiral refused to justify himself to a mere ship's captain—particularly a captain from the country that had spurned his great plan. He

Below: settlers in Haiti began sugar cultivation and this picture shows cane being cut. Production of sugar cane requires a large labor force and so was suitable for a slave economy.

Below: reproduction of a woodcut made in 1486 showing the artist's idea of the *Santa María*. There is a lack of contemporary information on what the ship really looked like and here the artist has simply reproduced a galley.

Below: the New World that Columbus
refused to recognize that he had
discovered, stretches far to the
north of the islands where he landed.
Our photograph from space shows the
continent of North America, with the
the Florida coast in the foreground.

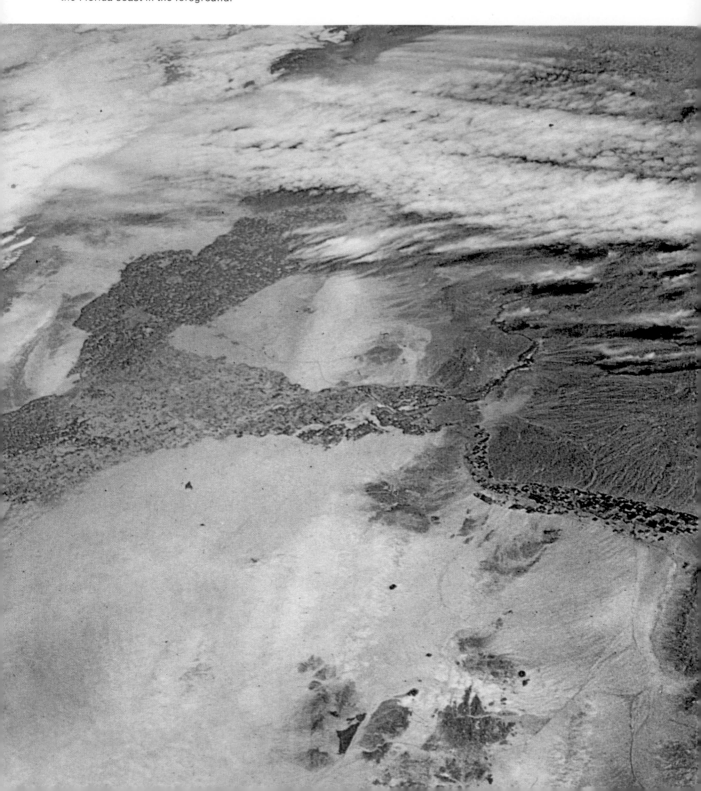

simply showed the man his credentials and then dispatched a letter to King John telling him about his voyage.

John, no doubt regretting his lost opportunity to sponsor the voyage, but nevertheless filled with admiration for the brave commander, invited Columbus to visit him at court. There the admiral was treated with every mark of respect. Despite this, he could not resist taunting the king with his success, and mocking him for having thrown away a claim to the wealth of "the Indies." In fact, so outrageous did Columbus' remarks become that John had to restrain his infuriated courtiers from murdering the admiral. John himself kept his temper for the time being. He honored Columbus, dressed his "Indian" natives in fine red cloth, and bade the admiral farewell.

It was March 15 before Columbus reached Palos, and late April before he arrived, by an overland route, at the court of Ferdinand and Isabella. The king and queen were overjoyed at the success of the voyage and the prospects it opened for trade with the Indies. In their gratitude to the brave Admiral of the Ocean Sea, they rewarded and honored him lavishly.

Columbus later undertook three more voyages across the Atlantic, and on all three made important new discoveries. He went on identifying them as Asian lands, however, because, to the end of his days, he believed that he had reached the Orient.

This fact, of course, does not in any way lessen the magnitude of Columbus' achievement. It merely adds further irony to the story of the man whose unswerving faith in himself, his "mission," and his own radical theories opened the way to the New World.

Right: fort at San João do Estoril built to guard the mouth of the Tagus, the longest river in the whole Iberian peninsula, the two branches of which end in a large tidal lake above Lisbon. Columbus swam to the port of Lisbon after the ship in which he was sailing was attacked and caught fire in 1476.

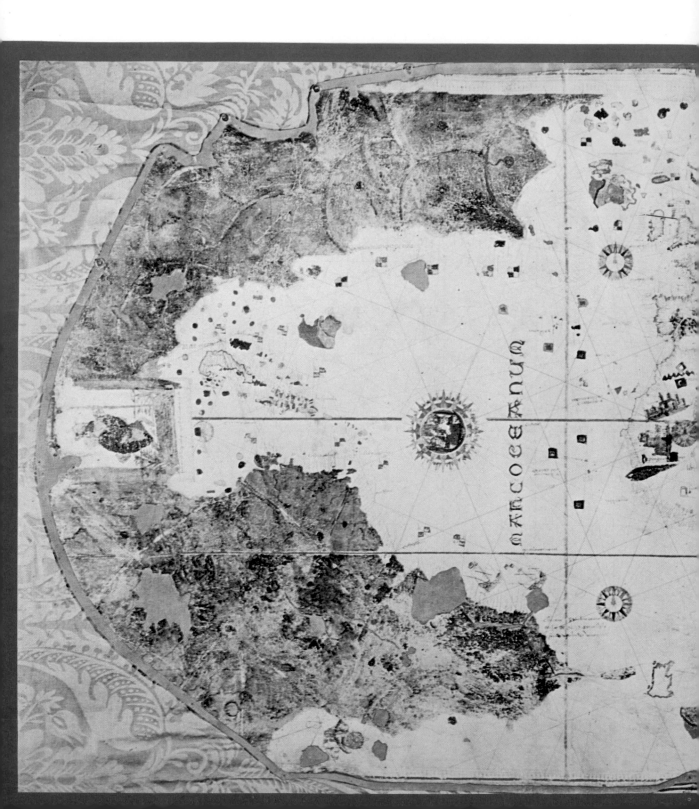

Below: this map of Juan de la Cosa was made in 1500 by Columbus' pilot and is the earliest known map showing the lands discovered by Columbus. The somewhat more accurate outlines of Europe, the Mediterranean Sea, and the African continent are shown in the badly faded center of the map. Also shown is possibly the first record of voyages made by Vincente Pinzón and John and Sebastian Cabot, and Vasco da Gama's arrival in India in 1498.

During his voyage across the Atlantic, Columbus had faced the gravest dangers with calm presence of mind. But at the court of King John he had been neither discreet nor diplomatic. However understandable his boasting may have been in the circumstances, it was exceedingly unwise. In fact, it almost started a war between Spain and Portugal.

It would have been better if Columbus, like Martin Pinzón, had sailed past Portugal to a Spanish port, and there sent a report to Ferdinand and Isabella. If King John had first heard details of the voyage from the Spanish monarchs, instead of from Columbus himself, he

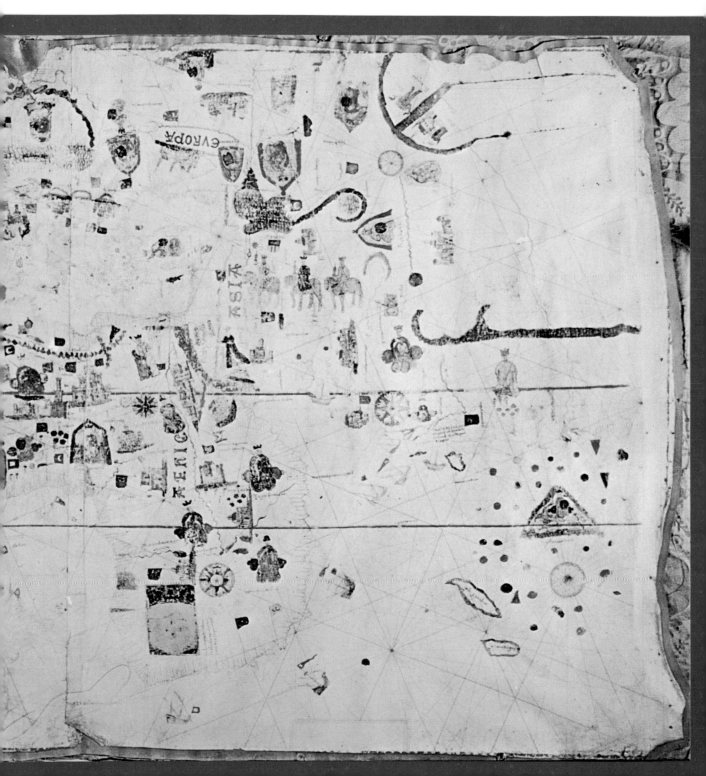

Right: this map of Haiti shows the location of Isabela, the city which Columbus established in Hispaniola. Unfortunately, because of the unhealthy location, the inhabitants of the city died and the city dwindled. There are virtually no traces left of it.

Above: Isabella la Católica (1451–1504), became queen of Castile in 1474 on the death of her brother. She married Ferdinand of Aragon in 1469. Her high intellect, fierce patriotism, and great religious conviction did much for Spain, raising it to the high standard it reached under "the Catholic rulers." Intuition led her eventually to agree to finance Columbus, and it is said she even offered to pawn her jewelry.

might possibly not have been as angry about the news as he now was.

Indeed, the admiral's impulsive boasting and taunting had so provoked King John that, within a few weeks of Columbus' visit, he was planning to send a fleet of his own across the Atlantic. He deeply resented Spain's entrance into the field of exploration and discovery. As far as he was concerned, Portugal had more than earned a monopoly over it. His plan, therefore, was to cut Spain out before it could make any further gains.

When Ferdinand and Isabella learned of John's proposed expedition, they set in motion the preparation of a war fleet. Meanwhile, having had Columbus' full report, they urged the Admiral to lead a second expedition before John could act.

Yet, even before Columbus had set out on his second voyage, the Spanish king and queen had already taken steps to ensure their rights in the western Atlantic. They had approached the pope—then the final arbiter in such affairs—and requested that Spain be given a monopoly over future transatlantic exploration. On May 3, 1493, the pope granted their request. Spain was to have sole rights to all discoveries made more than 100 leagues west of the Cape Verde Islands; Portugal was to have sole rights to all discoveries made east of that line of demarcation.

This arrangement did not please King John, and there followed a year of tense negotiations. Finally, on June 7, 1494, the two countries signed the Treaty of Tordesillas, which moved the line 250 leagues farther west. This new agreement (which ultimately gave Portugal rights to the part of South America now occupied by eastern Brazil) was more to John's liking.

Meanwhile, Columbus, accompanied by his brothers, Diego and Bartholomew, had embarked on his second expedition. This time the admiral was in command of 17 vessels. The fleet was too large for the little harbor of Palos. So it was from the port of Cádiz that, on September 25, 1493, the expedition set out. In addition to provisions, arms, ammunition, and horses, the ships carried various kinds of seeds, plants, and farm animals, because the main purpose of the expedition was to found a permanent colony in Hispaniola. All told, the fleet carried some 1,500 men. Among them were farmers, craftsmen, missionaries, doctors, and *hidalgos* (men of high birth accustomed to authority).

Columbus did not return from this expedition for nearly three years. During that time, he and his men discovered the islands of Dominica,

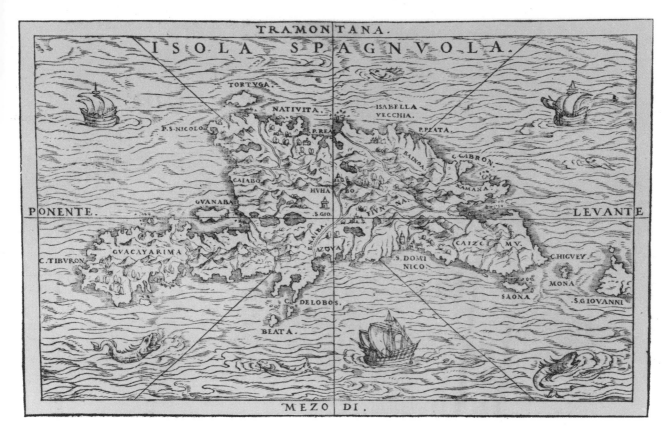

Guadeloupe, and Mariagalante (islands in the group known as the Lesser Antilles, southeast of Hispaniola), as well as Puerto Rico (due east of Hispaniola) and Jamaica (the island south of Cuba). They also further explored Cuba and Hispaniola, and they established the township of Isabela on its northern coast.

During these first fruitful years of Spanish exploration west of the Tordesillas line, Portuguese exploration east of it did not progress very rapidly. In fact, by 1496, when Columbus returned from his second voyage, the Portuguese had not advanced beyond the point reached by Bartolomeu Dias in 1488.

During this time, King John had been anxiously awaiting word from Pedro de Covilham, a man he had sent out at the same time as Dias. De Colvilham's mission was to sail to the eastern end of the Mediterranean, and from there to proceed overland in search of India and the land of Prester John.

De Covilham did, in fact, reach India, and even found on his way there an East African country ruled by a Christian king. This nation, which he took to be "the land of Prester John," was Ethiopia. It was some time, however, before the traveler was able to find a means of getting a letter back to Portugal. Thus, it was not until 1490 or 1491 that King John had a full report of De Covilham's movements.

In his letter, De Covilham described the busy trade in spices that he had witnessed in Calicut (modern Kozhikode) and Goa on India's west coast. He also said that if Portuguese ships could round the southern coast of Africa, they had only to sail a few hundred miles northward

Below: Prester John, the legendary Christian monarch of Asia, who combined the qualities of king and priest and ruled over huge domains somewhere in the Far East. His name was mentioned in ancient chronicles as early as 1122.

Above: Arab dhow of the type seen by Portuguese explorers as they sailed up the east coast of Africa. Dhows have sailed along this coast for centuries to and from Arabia. They sailed with the monsoon winds, which blow southwest for six months of the year and northeast for the other six months. These strange craft were a source of wonderment to the Portuguese, but it is certain that if the Portuguese found the Arabs and their vessels strange, then the Arabs found the Portuguese equally so.

along its east coast to the port of Sofala (midway along the coast of present-day Mozambique). There, he wrote, they would meet Arab ships which regularly voyaged to and from India. De Covilham's letter offered positive proof that the Atlantic merged with the Indian Ocean. The sea route to India lay ready for the taking, just as John had hoped.

But the report had reached the king at an inopportune time. John's son and heir had recently been killed in a riding accident, and the king himself was ill. Nevertheless, according to Gaspar Correa, a Portuguese historian of the period, John lost no time in preparing a fleet of ships to pioneer the ocean route to India. "He commanded timber to be cut down, which carpenters and shipwrights ordered for cutting, and the timber was brought to Lisbon, where three large ships were at once begun...."

But at this point, John found himself beset by annoyances and delays. Columbus arrived with the disturbing news that he had reached the Indies by sailing west, and Portugal and Spain almost came to blows over the rights to transatlantic exploration. All this was very trying for the ailing king. In October, 1495, less than two years after diplomatic bargaining had finally brought about the Treaty of Tordesillas, John died.

The throne passed to Manuel I, a distant relation of King John. He was later to become known as Manuel the Fortunate—and fortunate he certainly was. During his reign all the great schemes for Portuguese discovery that had been initiated by Henry the Navigator, nurtured by Alfonso V, and furthered by John II, reached fulfillment.

King Manuel worked hard to achieve that fulfillment. Only two months after his accession, he brought the voyage-to-India project before his royal council. The scheme he put forward had serious implications for Portugal. Clearly, a single expedition would be a waste of money unless it could be followed up by an all-out effort to secure a sizable share of the Eastern spice trade. But this would almost certainly lead to fighting with the Moslems who controlled this trade. There might also be trouble with the Venetian Republic, whose position as middleman in the spice trade would suffer if Portugal began obtaining spices direct from the East. Some councillors were, therefore, against the whole idea. But others were willing to accept the risks, and, backed by these bolder men, Manuel decided to go ahead with his scheme. Within a year he had appointed a leader for the first expedition—Vasco da Gama.

No one really knows how or why Da Gama was chosen. One contemporary chronicler says that the king, looking down from a balcony, happened to see him crossing a courtyard and took a whim to appoint him. Other accounts offer the more plausible suggestion that Da Gama, having served in previous expeditions, had already been earmarked for the post during John's reign. Apart from these scraps of doubtful information, we know about Da Gama only that he was the son of a government official in the town of Sines; that he had reached his middle or late thirties when he began his great journey; and that he knew enough about navigation to determine a ship's latitude.

It would not have mattered much if Da Gama had known nothing about navigation. This was a task he could leave to the excellent pilots he took with him—pilots who had earlier sailed with Dias. Da Gama's task as commander of the fleet was to steel his men to endure the hardships of a voyage that would be longer than any undertaken before. Beyond this, his mission was to establish friendly relations with Eastern rulers, to open the way for Portuguese merchants and missionaries.

On Saturday, July 8, 1497, Da Gama and the 170 men who were to sail with him walked in procession through the streets of Lisbon to the docks where his four ships lay at anchor. Priests and friars walked with them carrying lighted tapers, "and the people of the city followed, uttering responses to a Litany." Then the abbot of a monastery "made a general confession and absolved... those who might perish in this discovery or conquest." The absolution covered a few convicts under

Below: Vasco da Gama (1469?—1524), discoverer of the sea route to India, was born at Sines in Portugal. He was given command of the expedition to India in 1497.

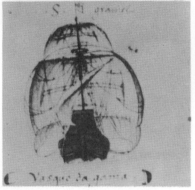

Above: ships specially built for Vasco da Gama's expedition to India, from a manuscript of 1497.

sentence of death, who were to be assigned duties of special danger during the voyage. Having received a final solemn blessing, the fleet then made ready to sail.

Like Columbus' vessels, Da Gama's ships seem terribly small by modern standards. His square-rigged flagship, the *St. Gabriel,* was of only about 200 tons. As was her sister ship, the *St. Raphael,* captained by Da Gama's brother Paulo. The *Berrio,* commanded by Nicolas Coelho, was a lateen-rigged caravel of some 100 tons. The fourth vessel, a store ship, was probably about 400 tons.

Bartolomeu Dias, who supervised the building of the *St. Gabriel* and the *St. Raphael,* had made sure they were of shallow draft, so that they could safely negotiate the shoals off the African coast. The smaller *Berrio,* similar to the caravels used by Henry the Navigator's pioneers, could certainly do so. But, as things turned out, Da Gama was to do very little "coast-hugging" along Africa's western shores.

The fleet had been at sea more than a week and was well south of the Canaries before the African coast was sighted. Then a dense fog closed down, and each vessel lost sight of the others. Another two weeks passed before they reassembled, far to the southwest, near the Cape Verde Islands. Here they agreed to put in for fresh provisions and drinking water. On August 3, they set off again, and followed a southeasterly course for some 800 miles.

After traveling this distance, Da Gama did something quite unheard of. He made a vast semi-circular sweep—first southwestward, then

Left: African villages, such as this one in Dahomey, have changed very little since the time of the early explorers, who found the way of life of the villagers quite incomprehensible. They therefore had great difficulty in deciding how best to treat the native peoples with whom they came into contact.

southeastward—through the Atlantic. It is said that he did so to avoid the doldrums and the awkward currents off the Gulf of Guinea, as well as the bad-weather area which Dias had encountered off southwest Africa. These considerations may have been in his mind, but there may also have been another. The Treaty of Tordesillas gave Portugal the right to explore as far as 350 leagues west of the Cape Verde Islands. Perhaps Da Gama made this westerly sweep through the Atlantic in the hope of finding undiscovered lands. He did not succeed in doing so, but it is interesting to note that, just before he crossed the Tropic of Capricorn, he was a good deal nearer to Brazil than he was to Africa.

During the course of that colossal westward sweep, Da Gama's men were out of sight of land for 96 days. As a result of going so long without fresh fruit and vegetables, many of them began to suffer from scurvy. So it was with joy and relief that at long last they found themselves within sight of land—St. Helena Bay, not far north of modern Cape Town. On November 4, even before landing at St. Helena Bay, they celebrated their good fortune by putting on their best clothes, flying flags, and firing the ships' cannons.

After so long a voyage, there was much work to be done—scraping barnacled hulls, mending torn sails, gathering provisions, filling the water-casks, and collecting wood for the cooking stoves. Meanwhile, some of Da Gama's pilots took an astrolabe ashore to determine the expedition's exact position. Used by a man standing on firm ground (rather than on the rolling deck of a ship), the instrument could give

Below: Bushmen, the nomadic hunters and food gatherers found by the Portuguese at the tip of the African continent. They are an entirely separate race of people, fairly short—the average height being only about five feet—with prominent cheekbones, broad noses and flat faces. Their short hair curls into small knots all over their heads.

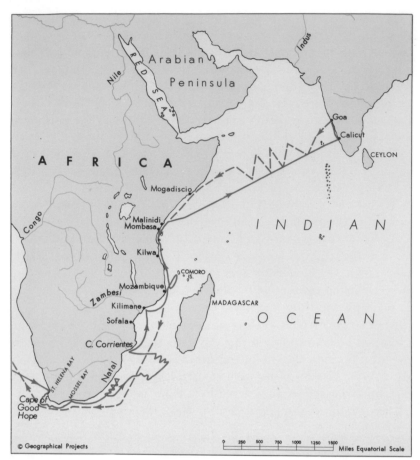

Right: the final part of Vasco de Gama's journey from Europe, crossing the Indian Ocean to the coast of India.

Below: an armlet and a horn or whistle made of ivory, the sort of things for which the Portuguese explorers traded with the inhabitants of the Ivory Coast. Ivory, the very dense substance of which elephant tusks are made, is very easy to work and the gelatinous solution with which it is filled gives it a wonderful polish. Elephants roamed over virtually the whole of the African continent for many years, but the Ivory Coast, between the Grain and Gold Coasts in West Africa, became a great trading center for ivory in the late 1400's.

fairly accurate results. It was not long before the pilots had fixed their latitude and calculated that they were about 120 miles north of the Cape of Good Hope.

Another inland excursion was not so profitable. One of the men took a few hours' leave to visit among the inhabitants of the region—Bushmen and Hottentots—whom the Portuguese had encountered for the first time on this voyage. He was invited to share a meal with the natives, but he must have done something to offend his hosts, for he soon found himself running for his life, with the natives in hot pursuit, throwing spears. He made it safely back to his ship, but Da Gama, who had gone to his rescue, was slightly wounded.

The expedition made several stops after leaving St. Helena Bay. On November 22, it rounded the Cape of Good Hope. A week later, it put in at Mossel Bay on the southern coast of Africa. There the men beached the store ship, broke her up, and distributed what remained of the stores among the other vessels. Meanwhile, Da Gama did some trading with the local inhabitants, exchanging little bells and scarlet caps for ivory bangles. In the course of his negotiations, he even managed to acquire an ox, which would provide fresh meat for his men. This bargaining was accompanied by much merrymaking. Everyone was dancing — the natives, the sailors, and Da Gama himself.

The stay in Mossel Bay lasted only until the necessary work had been

completed and the vessels restocked. Then the fleet sailed eastward
once more. By late December, it had reached and passed Algoa Bay,
the farthest point attained by Bartolomeu Dias. At last, Da Gama
was entering the Indian Ocean. Following the coastline, which now
curved northward, the fleet sailed on until Christmas Day, when it put
in to shore. Appropriately enough, Da Gama named the spot Natal.
Today, it is the great port of Durban, South Africa.

On leaving Natal, Da Gama turned eastward, away from the coast.
After several days, however, the fleet ran perilously short of fresh water,
and Da Gama was forced to sail west once more to reach the coast and
replenish supplies. He landed at the mouth of a small river and, while
the crew filled up the water-casks, did some trading with the local inhabitants, who paid in copper for the shirts he offered.

Next, after rounding Cape Correntes, near the Tropic of Capricorn,
Da Gama sailed almost due north. Had he kept close inshore, he would
have come to Sofala, the town mentioned by De Covilham as a port
of call for Arab ships on their way to and from India. Standing well
out to sea, however, Da Gama's fleet missed Sofala, and went on instead to Kilimane, a town several hundred miles north of it, in present-
day Mozambique. Kilimane was too small to be an Arab port of call,
so the Portuguese could learn nothing there about the sea route to India.
Nevertheless, the Kilimane stopover was a useful one for other reasons.

Above: these African houses, which
look very primitive, are nonetheless
skillfully adapted to the climatic
conditions. The grass thatch keeps
out rain and the overhang gives
shade to the immediate area around
the house. The open sides permit the
occasional cool breezes to keep the
temperature inside comfortable.

Above: in Renaissance Europe spices were more than just a pleasant flavor to vary what was undoubtedly a most monotonous diet. They were also used, without very much success, to preserve meat through the winter when there was no fresh fodder available to keep animals alive, and all slaughtering had to be done in the fall. It was partly to break the traditional Arab monopoly in the spice trade that led the Portuguese to their voyages of endurance.

Scurvy was beginning to take its toll among the crew, and the sick welcomed a few days' rest. In fact, the stopover at Kilimane lasted from late January to the end of February, 1498. At that time, with the crews rested and the ships repaired and restocked, the fleet set sail once more.

Following the coast northeastward, Da Gama's vessels reached, in early March, the port city of Moçambique, some 350 miles north of Kilimane. Here the citizens were not amazed—as they been in Kilimane—by the size of the Portuguese vessels. Arab trading ships had been regular visitors to Moçambique for a long time. For a long time too, Moçambique had been predominantly Moslem in its religion, for where the Arabs traveled, they also spread their faith. This city, 17° south of the equator, was as much a part of Islam as were the southern shores of the Mediterranean. In fact, as Da Gama was soon to find, the Moslem faith was on the increase almost everywhere in the area around the Indian Ocean.

The men of Moçambique at first took Da Gama's ships to be Arab trading vessels. The fact that their sails were made of cloth instead of matted palm leaves, their timbers joined by nails instead of leather thongs, made no difference. Never having seen any but Moslem ships, the people of Moçambique assumed that these unusual vessels hailed from a Moslem kingdom far away.

Accordingly, the local officials went on board and welcomed the Portuguese heartily. Through Arabic-speaking Portuguese interpreters, the officials talked freely to Da Gama about the other Arab vessels then in port. These vessels were laden, they said, with spices, gold, and precious stones. But Da Gama and his men had no wish to sail under false colors. They declared themselves Christians, enquired about Prester John, and requested pilots to guide them eastward to India.

This frank admission of their religion and objectives produced an immediate change in the attitude of the local officials. They did supply the pilots Da Gama had asked for, but gave them secret instructions to lead the Portuguese astray. Even before the fleet left port, one of the pilots, offering to take a party ashore for drinking water, tried to lead them into an ambush. Fortunately, the Portuguese were on their guard, and avoided being caught. But Da Gama had to fire his cannon before anyone on shore would allow his crew to fill their water-casks. This accomplished, the fleet left Moçambique in haste.

On April 7, Da Gama reached Mombasa, 800 miles north of Moçambique, in present-day Kenya. Here, after stating their religion and

their aims, the Portuguese once again met with opposition. Messengers posing as Christians were sent to Da Gama by the local ruler. They offered to supply him with whatever stores he needed, but their real mission was to lull him into a false sense of security and to lure his crews away from their ships. Da Gama was not taken in by their friendly overtures, however. That night, when an armed party attempted to board his ships by force, he and his men were ready for them. When the attack proved unsuccessful, the last Moslem pilots from Moçambique jumped overboard. On April 12, still without clues as to the best route to India, Da Gama left Mombasa.

The next stage of the voyage lasted only three days and brought better

Above: Mombasa, East Africa, where in 1498 Vasco da Gama once more met with hostility in his quest for a route to India. The old harbor shown here, still used by dhows and other native craft, is on the northeast of the coral island on which Mombasa is built and which is connected to the mainland by a bridge.

111

Left: this is the kind of potentate with whom the Portuguese first came into contact. The Arab lack of enthusiasm for the visitors was understandable. In the first place they represented a threat to the thriving Arab trade and secondly they could not have been the most elegant of figures after many months at sea.

luck: the capture of several Moslems from a small bark sailing just off shore. On reaching the next coastal town, Malindi (about 50 miles north of Mombasa), Da Gama entrusted one of these Moslems with a message for the local ruler. The burden of this message was that Da Gama wished to establish friendly relations and find pilots who could guide him to India. The Sultan of Malindi responded well. He let Da Gama know that he had nothing but goodwill for Portugal (although he had probably never heard of it before). He also sent presents, including a considerable quantity of spices—cloves, ginger, nutmeg, and pepper. In return, the Portuguese commander sent him three copper bowls, some bells, a piece of coral, a hat, and an overcoat.

Partly as a result of this friendly exchange—and partly by holding one of the sultan's own servants until matters were arranged to his satisfaction—Da Gama at last obtained what he most needed: a pilot who knew the way to India. Guided by this pilot, the fleet sailed northeast until May 18. On that day, it reached its goal. At long last, the dream of finding an eastern sea route to India had been fulfilled.

On May 21, the three ocean-battered vessels anchored off Calicut, a major port on India's southwest coast. Soon the fleet was approached by a number of native boats. The moment for direct negotiations with the East had arrived. But Da Gama was apprehensive about how the Indians would react to the arrival of foreign traders. He therefore entrusted the first step in the negotiations to one of the convicts who had been allowed to sail with him on condition that they undertook particularly dangerous jobs. The man was put on one of the native boats and taken ashore. There he was conducted to two Moslem traders who spoke Spanish. They were astonished to learn where he came from, and asked him what Portuguese vessels were doing so far from home. In reply, he summed up 80 years of Portuguese endeavor in a few short words. "We come," he said, "in search of Christians and spices."

Below: ancient Calicut, southwest India, the port at which Vasco da Gama landed in 1498. It was then a flourishing city, famed for cotton weaving. "Calico" originally meant cloth from Calicut. Da Gama tried unsuccessfully to set up a trading settlement there. Similar efforts were made two years later by Pedro Cabral, but again local hostility caused destruction of the colony. Da Gama returned in 1502 and completely devastated the city in revenge.

Right: an Indian prince surrounded by his ladies in attendance and with his gold cuspidor. This shows the sophistication and splendor of the East which so overwhelmed the Portuguese and which made Vasco da Gama so ashamed of the gifts which the king had given him for the princes and merchants, and which he he had to pretend were his own poor possessions.

Above: engraving by De Bry from Pigafetta's "Viaggio de Magagliones negli anni 1519/1522" (Journey of Magellan in the years from 1519–1522), showing Magellan using a globe and dividers to determine the position of his ship.

In fact, Da Gama's stated mission was to open the way for Portuguese trade and the spread of Christianity. But he had to return home with positive proof—hopefully in the form of spices—that Portugal could profit from the new-found route to India. Otherwise, there would be no point in sending merchants and missionaries there in future.

In his attempt to obtain spices, Da Gama found himself facing two serious obstacles. The first, of course, was the Moslem monopoly of trade with the East. Moslem traders bought their spices and precious stones on India's southwest coast and then sailed north with them to ports on the Red Sea or the Persian Gulf. The precious cargoes then passed into the hands of Moslem caravan traders, who took them overland to the shores of the Mediterranean, where they were purchased by Venetian and Genoese merchants. From India to the Mediterranean, therefore, the spices and gems of the East were handled exclusively by Moslem merchants. Naturally, any outsider's attempt to break into this monopoly would be greeted with dark suspicion and open hostility.

On the other hand, the Indian merchants in the Hindu states along the coast were as willing—in principle—to do business with Christians as with Moslems. But they were reluctant to risk offending their Moslem clients unless the Christians had something exceptional to offer in the way of trade.

Here was the second obstacle facing Da Gama in his quest for spices: he had nothing valuable to offer in return. He had brought with him only oil, honey, striped cloth, bowls, red caps, shirts, bells, and strings of coral. But while these might interest buyers in Malindi, they met only with contempt in Calicut. In fact, when offering them to the local spice merchants, Da Gama had to pretend they were not the goods provided by his king, but simply odds and ends that he, a poor traveler, had bought and paid for himself.

During his three-month stay in Calicut, Da Gama managed to obtain an audience with the region's wealthy Hindu ruler. At first, the only satisfaction he had from this man was permission to sell his own poor merchandise. There followed a number of unpleasant episodes in which the king of Calicut imprisoned some of Da Gama's men and the Portuguese captured some of the king's. At last, however, just before the fleet sailed, the Hindu ruler relented, and gave Da Gama a letter for King Manuel. In it, he wrote, "In my kingdom there is abundance of cinnamon, cloves, ginger, pepper, and precious stones. What I seek from your country is gold, silver, coral, and scarlet." The way for future trade was thus opened, and Da Gama could go home content.

The homeward voyage was marked by many hardships and perils. After sailing northward to Anjediva, an island south of Goa, the fleet struck out eastward for Africa in early October. Because of calms and contrary winds, the crossing to Mogadiscio (about 600 miles north of Mombasa, in present-day Somalia) took nearly three months. During this time, 30 crew members died of scurvy. Having at last reached the African coast in January, 1499, the fleet began the long southward voyage to the Cape of Good Hope. Along the way, several stops were made to take on water and provisions. On one of these stops, just south of Mombasa, the *St. Raphael* had to be destroyed because there were no longer enough men to handle three ships.

It was late March before the *St. Gabriel* and the *Berrio* eventually rounded the Cape. A month later, near the Cape Verde Islands, the two ships became separated. The *Berrio* sailed directly back to Portugal, but Da Gama, in the *St. Gabriel,* made a stopover in the islands. Thus, the leader of the expedition did not reach home until early September, 26 months after he had set out.

Da Gama was given a magnificent reception at King Manuel's court, and throughout the land his triumphant homecoming was marked by fetes and public rejoicings. Meanwhile, the wheels were set in motion for a full-scale program of eastward voyages. The time had come to capitalize on the hard-won sea route to the Indies.

Below: in the shadow of Table Mountain, at the southernmost tip of Africa, lies Cape Town, the oldest town in South Africa. It has grown from the tiny Dutch settlement founded in 1652 by the Dutch East India Company, to become the main passenger and mail port of South Africa. Da Gama's first landfall for over three months, after he left Cape Verde Islands in August 1497, was at St. Helena Bay, just north of present-day Cape Town.

Below: early map of Cochin, southern India. When in 1498 Da Gama reached the Malabar coast, the rulers of Cochin and Calicut were in conflict. Because Cochin harbor was superior to that at Calicut, the Portuguese sided with the Cochin rajahs. Dom Francisco de Almeida took up residence in Cochin when he became viceroy of Portuguese India in 1505.

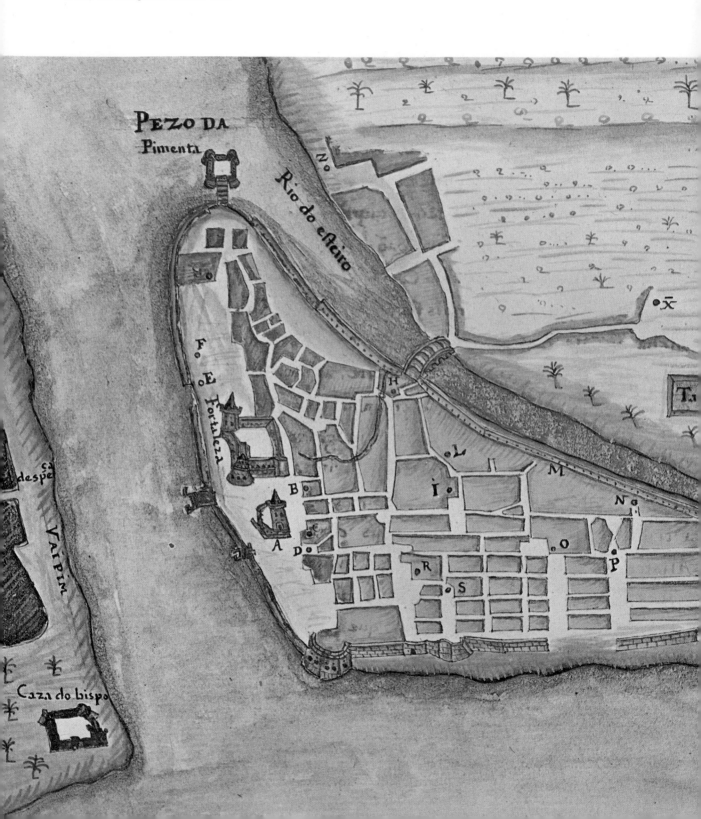

Thrusting East and West
7

During the early years of the 1500's, Da Gama's discovery of the ocean route to India was followed up with amazing speed and vigor. During the same period, Columbus' discovery of lands across the Atlantic was pursued with equal energy. But the results obtained by the two efforts were in striking contrast. The eastward thrust brought quick and prodigious results; the westward at first brought little but frustration.

On March 9, 1500, less than six months after Da Gama's return, a fleet of 13 well-armed ships laden with trading goods left Lisbon bound for the East. In overall command of the fleet was a nobleman, Pedro Álvares Cabral. With him were several captains, including Bartolomeu Dias and Nicolas Coelho, the captain of the *Berrio* on Da Gama's expedition.

On its way south, Cabral's fleet made a wide westward sweep through the Atlantic—like Da Gama's, but even wider. This tremendous sweep westward brought stunning results: the discovery of Brazil, on the eastern coast of South America. But despite this discovery, Cabral was anxious to get on to India. He did explore a considerable stretch of the Brazilian coast and left two men there to learn all they could about the people and natural resources of the area. Then, having sent one of his ships back to Portugal with the news of this new land, he sailed on.

Off the Cape of Good Hope, the fleet ran into a fierce storm and four ships were lost. (Among them was the vessel captained by Bartolomeu Dias, the first man to have reached the "Cape of Storms.") But the ships that reached India did very well. Because the fleet carried far better merchandise than Da Gama's, Cabral was able to trade more successfully with the ruler of Calicut. And because the fleet also carried better artillery, Cabral was able to attack Moslem vessels which tried to hinder his trading, and even seize their cargoes. Moreover, Cabral succeeded in making commercial treaties with the rulers of Cochin (south of Calicut) and Cannanore (north of Calicut). Cabral returned to Lisbon in July, 1501, his ships heavily laden with quantities of spices, as well as porcelain, incense, aromatic woods, pearls, diamonds, and rubies.

Cabral's remarkable success was soon repeated by many other Portuguese fleets. One of these was a powerful armada of 22 ships which carried several thousand men. This armada, which sailed in 1505, was under the command of Francisco de Almeida, who had been appointed Portugal's first viceroy in India. Under his direction the first permanent Portuguese forts were established in India.

By this time, Portugal was beginning to make a sizable dent in Islam's

Above: the Portuguese who reached India in the 1500's saw many boats like these along the Malabar coast. The Indians rarely sailed far from land. They relied on the Arabs for goods from a distance and this was one of the factors which, until then, had made the Arabs so important as middlemen.

monopoly of the spice trade. Soon after the Portuguese began sailing to India, the Moslem sea trade between India and ports on the Red Sea began to fall off noticeably. As a result, so too did the Moslem caravan trade between the Red Sea and the Mediterranean. This in turn affected the Venetian merchants who depended on the Moslems for the spices and other luxury items they marketed to the west. Helpless to reverse the trend, Venetian traders watched their cherished position as middlemen in the East-West trade slowly but surely being usurped by the Portuguese. Some far-sighted Venetian merchants even began transferring their capital from Venice to Lisbon.

Even Egypt felt the effects of Portugal's burgeoning trade with the East. As fewer and fewer Moslem caravans crossed her lands on their way to the Mediterranean, the vast revenues she had derived from taxing them rapidly diminished. In fact, Portugal's increasing use of the sea route to India was beginning to affect the whole pattern of world trade, and Lisbon, capital of this small but enterprising nation, was fast becoming a mecca for merchants from all over Europe.

But this was only the beginning. Having opened the way to the East, Portugal was not slow to strengthen her position there. In 1507 or 1508, a Portuguese fleet commanded by one Afonso d'Albuquerque conquered Hormuz, the port city that guarded the straits leading into the Persian Gulf. This action enabled the Portuguese to stop Eastern goods, brought to Hormuz in Moslem ships, from reaching the merchants who could take them overland through Moslem Syria to the Mediterranean. A year or two after the capture of Hormuz, Albuquerque, having succeeded De Almeida as Portugal's viceroy in India, also seized Goa, then probably the richest port on India's west coast.

Only one major step remained to be taken. India was not the source of spices, it was simply the place where they could be obtained in quantity at a reasonable cost. They actually originated in a group of islands much farther to the east. What Portugal now coveted was a foothold in these islands—islands, it was said, where every kind of valuable spice grew as abundantly as weeds in a neglected garden.

In 1511, Albuquerque sailed east to Malaya, the southernmost peninsula of Southeast Asia. On Malaya's west coast he seized the port of Malacca. This gave Portugal control over the narrow strait between the peninsula and Sumatra, the large island south and west of Malaya. It was through this strait that ships from the Spice Islands passed on their way to India.

The same year (1511), Albuquerque sent out an expedition to explore the Spice Islands themselves. These islands, which today are called the Moluccas, lie roughly midway between the Philippines and Australia. East of them lies the large island of New Guinea, and west, the smaller Indonesian island of Celebes. The vessels sent out by Albuquerque sailed nearly 1,000 miles beyond Java, the Indonesian island southeast of Sumatra, before it reached the tiny Moluccan island of Banda. Here they took on a fine cargo of cloves before setting sail for home.

The expedition of 1511 had failed to reach the richest Spice Islands, Ternate and Timor, which lie several hundred miles away from Banda. By 1520, however, the Portuguese had not only reached these islands, but sailed far north and west of them to China.

By 1520, also, the Portuguese had discovered and explored other lands in and around the Indian Ocean. Among these were Madagascar, off the coast of Mozambique; Ceylon, off the southern tip of India; and Burma, a large kingdom in the Bay of Bengal opposite India. Not only did the Portuguese establish trading stations in these far-flung places, they also often succeeded in forcing the local rulers to pay tribute to King Manuel I. As the fortunes of Portugal approached their zenith, the little nation's power in the Far East became so great that ships from other countries dared not sail into the Indian Ocean without written Portuguese consent.

While Portugal was reaping the tremendous rewards of her eastward expansion, Spain was vainly striving to make some sense—and profit—from her westward claims. In 1498, the year in which Da Gama first reached Calicut, Christopher Columbus made his third Atlantic voyage.

Above: Dom Francisco de Almeida, from a manuscript of the 1500's. Almeida was born in Lisbon in the mid-1400's and became first viceroy of Portuguese India. In March, 1505 he sailed for India, where he conquered Quiloa. He then went on to take Mombasa. In an attempt to maintain Portuguese supremacy, Almeida built forts at Anjediva, near Goa, and at Cannanore. He was killed in a fight with Hottentots on the site of present-day Cape Town in 1510.

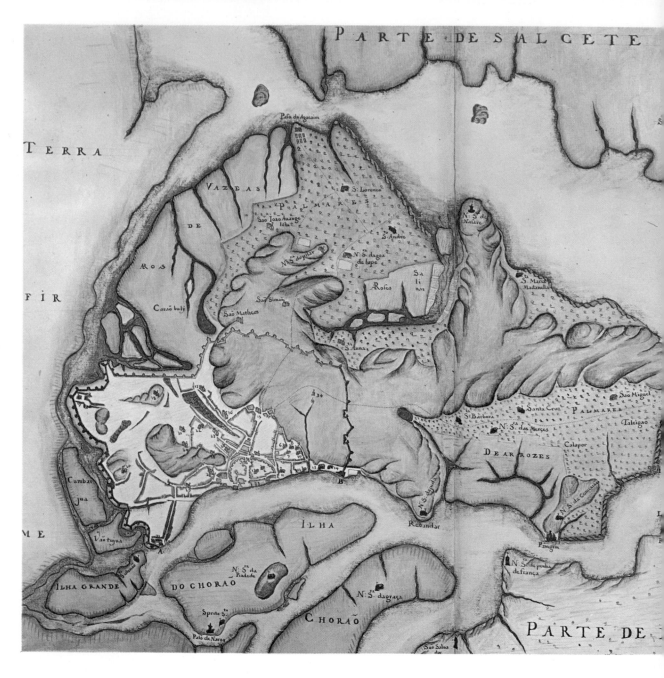

On the map, the following place names are visible:

PARTE·DE·SALCETE

TERRA

DE

VAZEAS

FIR

PALMARES

AROS

Pafo de Agaçaim

S. Lorenço

Sao João Auange lifta

S. Andre

N. S. das
de lupo

Rofes

Sa
linas

N. S. de
Nature

S. Maria
Madanela

N. S. do pilar

Carao buly

Sao Simao

Sao Matheu

S. Anna

Sao Miguel

Santa Cruz   PALMARES

S. Barbora

N. S. das Merces

Taleigao

DE ARROZES

Calapor

Cumbar
jua

ILHA

N. S. d ajuda

Rebandar

Pangim

N. S. da Conceiçao

N. S. de penha
de frança

Vas tujua

ME

ILHA GRANDE

DO CHORÃO

N. S. da
Piadade

N. S. da graça

PARTE DE

Sprito S.

CHORÃO

Pafo de Naroa

Sao Salva
dor

Above: an old map of Goa, the city seized by Afonso d'Albuquerque in the early 1500's. Goa was the first Portuguese territorial possession in Asia and became the capital of the Portuguese eastern empire, reaching its height of prosperity between the late 1500's and early 1600's. After this it declined and in the 1800's only a handful of priests, monks, and nuns lived there.

On this voyage, the Admiral of the Ocean Sea discovered and named the island of Trinidad, a few miles off the coast of present-day Venezuela. Strangely enough, though he sailed along the Venezuelan coast as far as the mouth of the Orinoco River, he did not make a landing on the mainland. Instead, he hastened northward to inspect the new colony at Hispaniola. He found it in a state of revolt. He and his brothers, Diego and Bartholomew (who had been given major responsibilities in governing the colony), handled the situation badly, being sometimes too lenient, sometimes too quick to resort to the whip and the gallows.

News of this trouble in Hispaniola soon reached the ears of Ferdinand

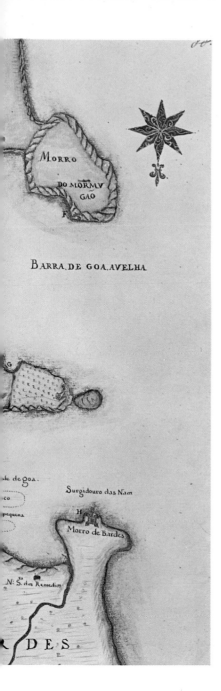

MORRO

DO MORMV GAO

BARRA DE GOA AVELHA

de de goa

Surgidouro das Naos

pequena

Morro de Bardes

N.ᵃ S. des Remedios

DES

Right: illustration showing a clove tree, from Pigafetta's *Relation*, an account of Magellan's first circumnavigation, written in 1524 by Antonio Pigafetta, a volunteer in Magellan's flagship. Pigafetta stressed the interest shown in the clove tree and the desirability of cloves in trading. A native of the Moluccas, or Spice Islands, the clove tree is an evergreen, growing to a height of 15 to 30 feet. It has large oval leaves, and groups of crimson flowers at the tips of its branches.

and Isabella. To investigate the charges of cruelty and mismanagement against Columbus, they sent representatives of the crown to Hispaniola. Whether or not these charges were fully justified, it was apparent that Columbus made a better admiral than he did a governor. In October, 1500, he was arrested in Hispaniola, ignominiously brought back to Spain in chains, and stripped of his honors and privileges.

By May, 1502, however, he had partially restored himself to the good graces of his sovereigns, and was allowed to undertake another voyage with four Spanish vessels. Because he had been forbidden to visit Hispaniola, he confined his travels to the area south and west of it. For most of the two years of this voyage, he cruised along the east coast of Central America, from present-day Honduras to Panama. He still believed, of course, that he was on the threshold of Asia. In a letter to Ferdinand and Isabella describing this, his last voyage, he wrote, "On May 13 I arrived in Mango province, which is next to Cathay."

Four years after completing this voyage, Columbus died, never having learned the real truth about his discoveries. Perhaps it is as well that he did not. He had set his heart on reaching the Orient; to have known that he had found something quite different—no matter how

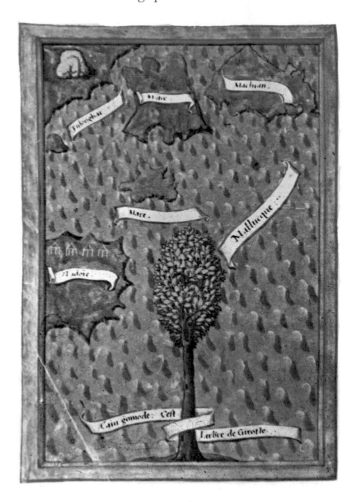

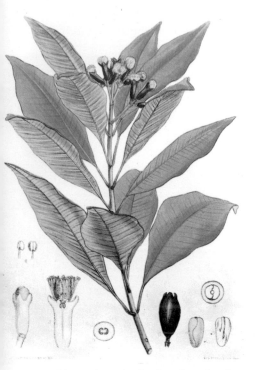

Above: branch of a clove tree showing details of buds, flowers, fruit, etc. The clove is the dried, unopened flower bud, which has a very powerful odor and hot taste. It has long been a very desirable spice for trading.

significant the discovery—would have been a cruel disappointment.

In any case, no one at this time possessed sufficient geographical knowledge to say with certainty that the admiral's discoveries were not what he said they were. In fact, until the last years of Columbus' life, few Europeans had any idea of what the real Orient was like. If Columbus saw some vague resemblance between the lands he discovered and the fabulous East described by Marco Polo, who could say he was wrong?

Yet, although Spain continued to call its transatlantic possessions "the Indies," some men had their doubts from the start. One such man was Peter Martyr, an Italian whose enormous correspondence on many subjects was to make him famous. Martyr had seen the natives of Guanahani that Columbus had brought home from his first voyage. The appearance and language of these natives did not agree with Martyr's ideas of how Orientals should look or speak. From May, 1493, onward he wrote numerous letters concerning Columbus and his discoveries, and in one, dated October, 1494, he called the admiral the discoverer of a "New World."

A decade or so after this observation, when the Portuguese were making regular voyages to the East, men were better able to compare Columbus' discoveries with the real Orient. It then became clear that the Admiral of the Ocean Sea had indeed placed a "New World" within Spain's grasp.

Meanwhile, Spanish exploration and colonization around the Caribbean Sea and the Gulf of Mexico were proceeding apace. In 1502, Nicolas de Ovando became governor of Hispaniola. He encouraged large numbers of Spaniards to make their homes there by offering them grants of land and Indian slaves to work it, provided they promised to stay in the island for at least five years. Hispaniola soon prospered under this scheme of colonization.

In 1509, Ovando was succeeded by Columbus' son Diego, who quickly embarked on an ambitious program of expansion. Within months of taking office he sent out an expedition under Alonso de Ojeda to found two new settlements. One of these was in present-day Colombia on the northern coast of South America. The other was just west of it, on the narrow Isthmus of Panama.

Some years after the first settlers arrived in Panama, governorship of the tiny colony passed into the hands of one Vasco Núñez de Balboa. It was he who, in 1513, first gazed out on the great ocean we call the

Above: Trinidad, the most southerly island in the West Indies, the point from which exploration of the rest of the New World began after Columbus' discovery in 1498. Most of the larger West Indian islands were settled by the Spanish in the 1500's. They oppressed the native inhabitants, forcing them into slavery in the fields and mines, and this lasted until the British, Dutch, and French freed them in the late 1800's.

Left: a woodcut made in 1502, from the Journal of Christopher Columbus, showing the presentation of a book to Ferdinand and Isabella. It was in the late 1400's that Columbus started sending his long letters of woe, protesting his supposed mistreatment, to his king and queen.

Left: pearl fishing in America, from an engraving by De Bry in 1594. Pearls found in Caribbean waters were one of the first signs of riches in the New World, other than the few gold ornaments Columbus found on the island of Hispaniola.

Left: in Marco Polo's account of the riches of Cathay, pearl fishing was also mentioned, as shown in this manuscript of 1338, from Les Livres de Graunt Caam. It was this sort of similarity that Columbus clutched at in his determination to believe that he had indeed reached Cathay. Bodleian Library MS Bodley 264. fol. 265.

Pacific. The discovery of an ocean stretching away to the west was completely unexpected. Balboa himself could form no conception of the extent of this immense "South Sea." But he did what any good Spaniard would have done in his place. He took formal possession of it for Spain.

Meanwhile, Don Diego was pursuing his expansionist policy in another direction. In 1511, he sent out 300 men from Hispaniola, under the leadership of Diego Velásquez, to conquer and settle Cuba. The conquest of the islanders was easily accomplished, and within a few years Cuba possessed nearly as many Spanish settlers as Hispaniola itself.

It was not long before Velásquez was sending out expeditions of his own. One, led by Francisco Hernandez in 1517, explored the north and west coasts of Yucatán, the bulge of land on Central America's east coast stretching toward Cuba. On this expedition Spaniards in the New World had their first encounter with Indians of an advanced culture. Those they met in Yucatán were not only well clad and well armed, but also proficient builders in stone.

A second expedition was sent out by Velásquez in 1518. Under the command of Juan de Grijalva, it followed the Central American coast many miles westward beyond Yucatán to present-day Mexico. Near where the Mexican city of Veracruz now stands, Grijalva's men encountered Indians whose manner and appearance clearly showed that they were men of wealth and high civilization.

Grijalva's expedition was to have momentous consequences both for Spain and for the world, since it led directly to Hernando Cortes' conquest of Mexico. But in 1518 that great event, which was to make Spain the envy of all Europe, still lay in the future. Meanwhile, all that Spain had thus far gained from the discoveries of Christopher Columbus and his successors was a few scattered farming colonies. While these settlements were not to be despised, they could bear no comparison with the mighty trading empire Portugal had built up in India and southeast Asia.

Nevertheless, Spain maintained a jealous watch over her transatlantic possessions. In the Caribbean and the Gulf of Mexico she had assembled enough ships, men, and arms to make other European nations very reluctant to trespass on her preserves. But it was well known that Spain was unprepared to protect her claims in the regions north and south of the Caribbean. As a result, ships and men from other Euro-

Above: the Panama Canal. World shipping now passes across the narrow neck of land that separates the Pacific Ocean from the Caribbean Sea. The isthmus twists in such a peculiar way that the opening to the Caribbean is actually west of the opening to the Pacific. Alonso de Ojeda founded a colony at Panama, at the southern end of the Canal, in 1499.

pean nations began to travel northwest or southwest across the Atlantic to try their fortunes in other parts of the New World.

It was in 1497 that England first joined in the scramble for overseas territories. Interestingly enough, it was not an Englishman, but a Venetian named John Cabot who sailed the first English ship to the New World. Cabot was living in England when he heard of Columbus' discoveries. John Cabot, with his son Sebastian, set out from Bristol to see if he, too, could find his way to "the Indies." Following a westerly course, he reached Cape Breton Island, off the northern coast

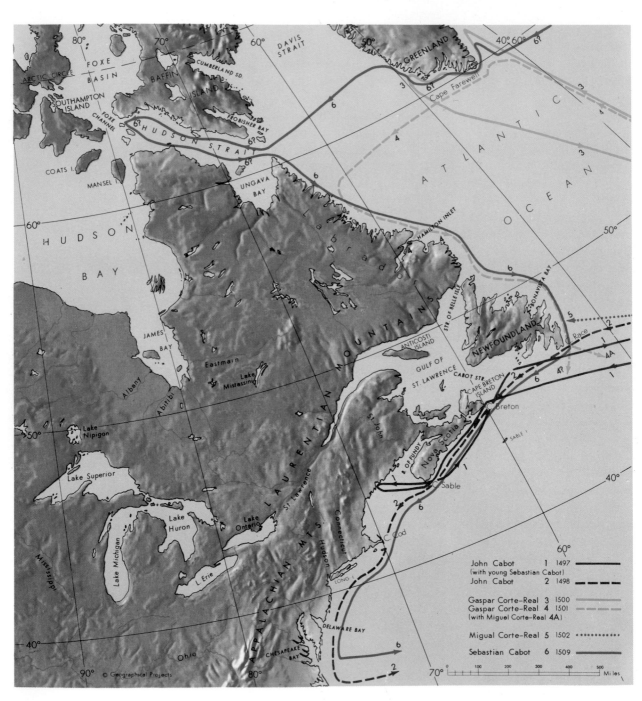

John Cabot	1	1497	
(with young Sebastian Cabot)			
John Cabot	2	1498	
Gaspar Corte-Real	3	1500	
Gaspar Corte-Real	4	1501	
(with Miguel Corte-Real 4A)			
Miguel Corte-Real	5	1502	
Sebastian Cabot	6	1509	

© Geographical Projects

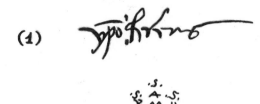

(1)

(2) XPO FERENS

(3)

Above: Christopher Columbus' signature. Prior to 1492 he signed himself "Christoferens", which he spelt "Xoferens." After the discovery of America he called himself "Al Almirante."

of Nova Scotia. He then sailed northeast to the larger island of New-foundland. Having cruised along its southern coast, he returned to England, where he announced that he had found the land of the Great Khan.

The next year, with the blessing and financial backing of England's King Henry VII, Cabot made another journey, this time without his son. He sailed northwest until he reached the coast of Greenland. Then he sailed southward along the shores of Labrador (on Canada's extreme northeast coast) to Nova Scotia. From here he continued south, and possibly had even reached Delaware Bay, more than halfway down the coast of North America, before he sailed for home.

Cabot's was a magnificent voyage, but it produced no spices and no ambassadors from the Great Khan. Disappointed, the English king lost interest in westward exploration. Sebastian Cabot, however, did not. In 1509, he set out once more from Bristol and, according to contemporary accounts, succeeded in sailing through Hudson Strait into Hudson Bay before returning home.

Meanwhile, Portugal, too, was developing an interest in northwest exploration. King Manuel had no wish to break the Treaty of Torde-sillas, of course. But no one knew precisely where the Tordesillas line of demarcation really was, because it was difficult to fix longitude at sea. For this reason, Manuel felt fairly safe in sending Portuguese ships quite a long way west.

Early in 1500, a man called Gaspar Corte-Real, who had probably heard of John Cabot's alleged discovery of the land of the Great Khan, applied to King Manuel for permission to go exploring in the north-west Atlantic. His petition was granted, and that very year he visited the east coast of Greenland, rounded Cape Farewell on its southern tip, and cruised a short distance northwest along its western coast before icebergs forced him to sail back to Lisbon. On this voyage he had the distinction of becoming possibly the first European (other than the Vikings) to meet Eskimos.

The next year, in command of three ships, Corte-Real sailed again, taking his brother Miguel with him. Together they visited Greenland, crossed the Davis Strait to Labrador, and sailed on down the coast of Newfoundland as far as modern Bonavista on its northeast coast. Then, while Gaspar Corte-Real continued southward, Miguel return-ed to Portugal with a number of natives captured in Labrador. Months passed and Gaspar failed to appear. Finally, in May 1502, Miguel sailed

Left: voyages made by the Cabots and the Corte-Reals to those parts of the New World safely north of Spanish claims. Only the green coastal areas were explored at this time.

northwest again in search of him. Nothing was ever heard of either brother again.

In 1520, another Portuguese mariner, one João Alvares Fagundes, explored the Atlantic coast from Nova Scotia to Placentia Bay in southeast Newfoundland. The following year he was granted permission to establish a colony in the islands along that coast.

The Cabots, the Corte-Reals, and Fagundes were but a few of the many adventurous men who explored the North Atlantic coast in the early 1500's. As these explorers learned more about the extent of the coast, it gradually became clear that, if ever men were to succeed in sailing west to Asia, they must somehow find their way around a huge continental landmass. It also became clear that any attempt to find a "northwest passage" through the waters of the Arctic Ocean would be extremely difficult, if not downright impossible.

What of trying to reach the Indies by sailing *south*westward? Ultimately, the search for a southwest passage around the tip of South America was to produce one of history's most spectacular voyages: the first circumnavigation of the globe. But that voyage still lay two decades away when, in 1498, the great southern landmass was first sighted by Christopher Columbus. The admiral did not know, of course, what he had discovered when he sailed along the coast of Venezuela. But he did make a rough map of that coast to show the location of the island of Trinidad.

Right: this central American Aztec figure of about A.D. 1500 shows the sophisticated civilization which the Spanish stumbled upon when exploration of the New World got under way.

Left: John Cabot, born in Venice in 1450, leaving Bristol in 1497 carrying letters patent from Henry VII of England. These granted John and his three sons, Lewis, Sebastian, and Santius, "full and free authority, leave and power upon theyr own proper costs and charges, to seeke out, discover and finde whatsoever isles, countries, regions or provinces of the heathen and infidels, which before this time have been unknown to all Christians." They reached Newfoundland before returning to England.

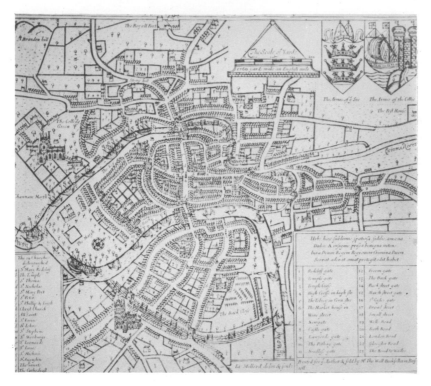

In 1499, a man who had seen that map set out with four small ships to explore the region. This man was Alonso de Ojeda, who later established the colony at Panama. On his 1499 voyage to South America, he took with him a middle-aged Florentine businessman named Amerigo Vespucci. Ojeda and Vespucci sailed to a point on the South American coast near Cape St. Roque on the northeastern tip of Brazil. They then followed the coast westward, far beyond Trinidad to the Gulf of Venezuela, before returning home.

In 1499, Vincente Pinzón, captain of the *Niña* on Columbus' first voyage, sailed to the South American coast and reached Cape St. Roque, a point on the eastern bulge of Brazil. He then proceeded northwest along the coast to the mouth of the Amazon River.

Did Pinzón reach Brazil before April, 1500, when Cabral's westerly sweep through the Atlantic brought him to those shores? Considering that Pinzón set out in 1499, it seems likely that he did, a fact which would give the honor of the discovery to Spain rather than Portugal. But, in fact, the whole question is shrouded in mystery. Many historians believe that the Portuguese knew of the existence of the Brazilian coast several years *before* Cabral reached it. Indeed, some say that it was for this reason that King John II insisted on having the pope's demarcation line moved farther west by the Treaty of Tordesillas. Certainly, it is well known that Portugal tended to keep her discoveries to herself, so the theory may well be correct.

In any case, both Spain and Portugal knew of Brazil by the middle of the year 1500. And, under the Treaty of Tordesillas, both had some claim to explore South America's east coast. Many men were to take part in this exploration during the next few years, and their discover-

Right: ice floes at Kap Dan, Greenland, the largest island in the world, the major part of which is within the Arctic Circle. John Cabot passed the island on his second voyage in 1498 when he reached North America.

Below: the four voyages of Columbus and Vespucci's travels in the Caribbean.

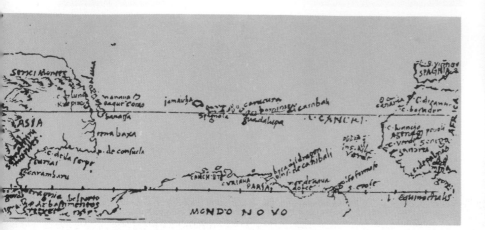

Above: sketch based on a map by Bartholomew Columbus, showing his idea of the world. Spain and Africa can be seen on the right, with the islands of Jamaica, Hispaniola, and Guadelupe in the middle between Africa and Asia. South of these islands is an enormous continent called Mondo Novo—new world.

ies were soon to lead them farther south than Europeans had ever traveled.

In 1501, Portugal's King Manuel sent out an expedition to determine how large "Brazil" was, and whether there was a way around it which could be used to reach the Indies. Amerigo Vespucci, now in the service of Portugal, took part in the expedition. (He was not an experienced seaman, but doubtless his business acumen was considered useful in drawing up a report on the resources of the land, so far as could be judged from the coast.) Little is known about what this expedition accomplished, except from the pen of Vespucci himself, and he says that the fleet followed the coast as far as latitude 50° S—only 400 miles from the extreme southern limits of the continent. Few people accept this statement as true. But, from snippets of information left by others who took part in the voyage, it seems likely that the expedition did reach latitude 32° S, near the present boundary between Brazil and Uruguay. Vespucci's writings and extravagant claims later made him famous, and his Christian name, Amerigo, was used in naming both of the great continents in the New World. Nevertheless, few historians today believe that he did half as much exploring as he claimed to have done.

The next really vital step in South American exploration was an indirect one. It came in 1513, when Balboa first gazed on the "South Sea." Although no one yet knew the extent of this new-found ocean, many men guessed—and rightly—that it extended the whole length of western America's shores and provided a way west to the Orient.

With Balboa's tantalizing "South Sea" in mind, adventurous mari-

Above: Bay of Alcantara, near the mouth of the Amazon River. The mighty Amazon—though no one at the time realized just how massive it is—is the great South American river which Vincente Pinzón discovered in 1500. He called it the "Rio Santa Maria de la Mar Dulce," but after its first descent from the Andes in 1541 by Orellana, he gave it the name "Amazonas" after a battle with savages in which the women of the tribe also took part.

Right: Amerigo Vespucci (1451—1512), who gave his name to America, was born in Florence and became a Spanish subject in 1505. He made several conflicting claims of journeys for Spain and Portugal, in one of which, in 1497, he said that he had discovered a new continent, or the New World. Columbus, still imagining that he had reached the Indies, did not dispute Vespucci's claim. The suggestion that the new continent, which was in fact South America, be given Vespucci's name was adopted, for South, and later North, America.

Right: the mouth of the River Plate, on the eastern side of South America, which Juan de Solís entered in 1515 in the hope of finding a passage from the Atlantic to the "South Sea," discovered the year before by Balboa. De Solís was ambushed and killed by Charrua Indians in 1515. The river was given the name Río de la Plata (silver) by Sebastian Cabot in 1526 after he had bartered with the Guarani Indians for silver ornaments.

ners became more anxious than ever to find a southwest passage to India. Spaniards in particular became obsessed by the idea, for Spain's possessions in the New World were still not paying very high dividends. If they could find a westward route to the South Sea, they could reach the Spice Islands and challenge Portugal's hold on the East.

It was probably with this object in view that Juan de Solís, a Portuguese pilot working for Spain, sailed southwest to the Bay of Rio de Janeiro in 1515. He continued south from this bay until he reached the enormous Río de la Plata estuary, in modern Uruguay. As De Solís sailed west into this estuary, he found that the water continued

to be salty for many miles. Possibly, therefore, he mistook it for a strait
that would lead directly to the South Sea. It was a natural mistake, but
it proved fatal for De Solís and some of his men. Some way along the
banks of the great river, he and eight others went ashore and were captured and killed by cannibals.

Sometime after the survivors of this expedition returned to Portugal,
word of De Solís' "strait" to the South Sea reached the ears of an ambitious Portuguese mariner named Fernão de Magalhães. The remarkable voyage he made in pursuit of this strait was one day to make him
famous the world over as Ferdinand Magellan.

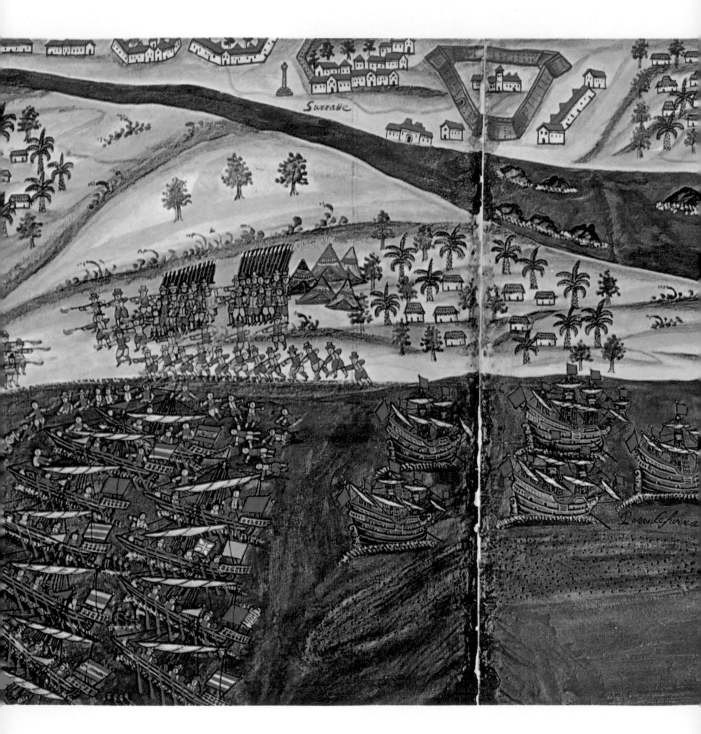

Around the World
8

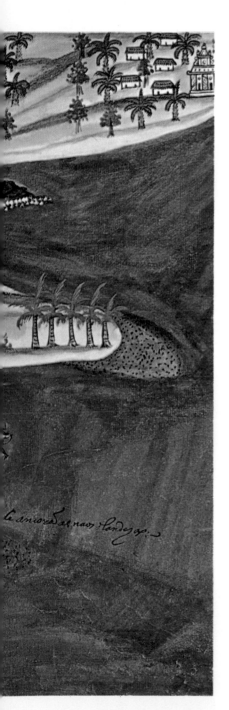

Ferdinand Magellan was born at Sabrosa, in central Portugal, in 1480. His father was one of the less important nobles, and at an early age he became a page in the court of King John II. At 15, he entered the service of John's successor, Manuel I, as a soldier. During the next few years he served on many of the most important of Portugal's first expeditions to the east, and gradually rose in rank.

In 1505, he sailed to India with the great armada of Francisco de Almeida, and was wounded at the battle of Cannanore. He was sent to Sofala, on the African coast, and helped build the first Portuguese fort there. He returned to India, and in 1509 took part in a naval battle against a Moslem fleet off Diu. Later that year, he signed on with the fleet which made the first Portuguese visit to Malaya. This expedition nearly met with disaster. When the Portuguese arrived on the Malay coast, they were greeted with apparent friendliness by the Sultan of Malacca. The welcome he extended, however, was only a trick to disarm the Portuguese. The sultan sent many of his men, secretly armed, to the Portuguese ships in the guise of "traders." Meanwhile, he invited boatloads of the crew ashore to pick up cargo. Suddenly, a signal was given, and the Portuguese were simultaneously attacked on land and sea.

In this dangerous situation, Magellan distinguished himself by

Left: battles between the invading Portuguese, who intended to set up trading compounds, and Arabs, who naturally wanted to protect their monopoly, were frequent. Magellan took part in such a battle early in his career. This particular battle shown was at Surat in Gujurāt, just north of Bombay, India.

Right: Ferdinand Magellan (1480—1521), captain of the expedition which first circled the globe. He made many voyages for Portugal, but, after losing favor with King Manuel, he went to Spain. In 1519 he sailed westward from Spain to find a route to the Spice Islands, on the way discovering the passage from the Atlantic to the Pacific which now bears his name. He was killed in a fight on the island of Mactan in the Philippines.

Below: a fleet of Portuguese carracks such as that in which Magellan sailed to India in 1505 under the command of Francisco de Almeida.

Right: close-up of sailors working on the topmasts of one of the ships.

calmness and bravery. Even before the Malays attacked, he suspected danger and was able to warn his captain in time to save his life and the lives of his crew. One chronicler also relates that Magellan saved another man, Francisco Serrão, who was among the party of men ashore. When the attack began, Magellan, it is said, rowed ashore and rescued Serrão, who thereafter became his lifelong friend.

In 1510, Magellan sailed with a ship bound for Portugal. Off the Laccadive Islands, to the west of Calicut, the ship went aground on a reef and broke up. The ship's boat could hold only a few men, and the officers (of whom Magellan was one) decided to sail them back to India to procure a rescue ship. When the rest of the crew learned that they were to be left behind, they nearly mutinied. Magellan prevented this mutiny by volunteering to remain behind with them.

Back in India once more, Magellan was rewarded for his services with the rank of captain. The following year he again distinguished himself in the Portuguese conquest of Malacca, led by Afonso d'Albuquerque. He then took part in the first Portuguese expedition to the Moluccas, late in 1511. His friend Francisco Serrão was also on this expedition. But after the ships had filled their holds with cloves at the tiny island of Banda, Serrão's ship was wrecked. Fortunately, Serrão

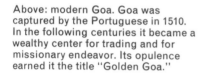

Above: modern Goa. Goa was captured by the Portuguese in 1510. In the following centuries it became a wealthy center for trading and for missionary endeavor. Its opulence earned it the title "Golden Goa."

was rescued by some islanders, and taken to the island of Ternate. When later voyages brought the Portuguese to Ternate, Serrão chose to remain on the island. Via Portuguese merchants he began to send letters to his friend Magellan describing the riches of the islands and urging him to make a voyage there. These letters were to play a significant part in Magellan's decision to pioneer a southwest route to the East.

Meanwhile, Magellan's status as captain had had one unfortunate result. In 1510, Albuquerque called together all his captains to ask them whether or not they agreed that the rich Indian port of Goa should be attacked then or in a year's time. He hoped, of course, that they would all agree to the launching of an immediate attack. Most did, but not Magellan; he urged that the overworked crews be given a rest before undertaking so arduous a campaign.

Some historians suspect that Albuquerque reported unfavorably on this incident to King Manuel. They may well be right, for when Magellan returned to Portugal in 1512, he found himself distinctly out of favor with the king. The way in which Manuel showed his displeasure was by not increasing the pension which Magellan, like all members of the Portuguese nobility, regularly received from the crown. At that time an increase in pension was the customary way of honoring a nobleman who had distinguished himself in the king's service. But on his return to Portugal—after serving bravely in numerous campaigns and expeditions abroad—Magellan received no increase whatsoever. Instead, he was given barely enough to enable him to live in Portugal in genteel poverty. So, after a year, he volunteered for active service once more. He took part in a Portuguese attack on Morocco and, in the fighting, received a lance wound that left him with a permanent limp. But that was not the worst of his luck. Some of the stores he was in charge of disappeared, and he was accused of misappropriating them.

BORNE

EQVINOCTIAL:
MOLLVQVES:

TIMOR:

ANDE:

Without awaiting trial—and without obtaining leave—Magellan made his way home to protest his innocence to the king. Although it was obvious from Magellan's previous record that he was a man of honor, Manuel refused to listen to a man who had technically deserted. He sent Magellan back to Morocco to stand trial.

The trial cleared Magellan of all suspicion, but that no longer satisfied him. In Manuel's service he had not only been unjustly accused, but also insufficiently rewarded. It was not enough to be cleared of what he had *not* done; he also wanted recognition for what he *had* done.

Again Magellan went to the king. This time he made three requests. First, he asked for an increased pension as a token of royal esteem. The king refused. Second, he asked to be assigned a mission through which he might gain the king's respect and confidence. Again the king refused. Finally, he asked if he might seek service under some other monarch. To this, the king in effect replied, "Do as you please."

Hurt and annoyed by the king's disinterest, Magellan began casting about for some means by which he could win the honors that had so far eluded him. He made regular visits to the royal library, where maps and charts of the latest discoveries were kept. He had frequent talks with one Ruy Faleiro, a mapmaker who firmly believed that there was a strait between the Atlantic and the Pacific somewhere near latitude 40°S (several hundred miles south of the Plate estuary). And he pored over his letters from Francisco Serrão urging him to visit the Moluccas. Slowly Magellan began to formulate an adventurous scheme that would bring him fame and profit. He would find the strait Faleiro spoke of (and that Juan de Solis had died in search of in 1516) and sail west to the Spice Islands.

No one knew whether the Spice Islands lay in the part of the world to which Portugal had rights or in the part to which Spain had rights. The Treaty of Tordesillas had divided the world equally between Por-

Above: detail of a world map made for Henry II of France in the 1500's, showing the Moluccas, or Spice Islands. Spain claimed the islands under the Treaty of Tordesillas, but Portugal bought them in 1528 and they remained Portuguese possessions until the early 1600's when the Dutch took them over.

Above: a dish and a covered cup made of Portuguese silver-gilt, the sort of articles that would have been in use in Portuguese court circles in the 1400's and early 1500's.

Right: the *Victoria*, the only survivor of the five vessels which sailed under Magellan in 1519. Only 17 men were on board the sorry-looking ship which returned to Spain three years later, but the information that they brought back about the journey was of unaccountable value to world history.

tugal and Spain. Therefore, at some point 180° east of the Tordesillas line, Portugal's rights must end and Spain's begin. But because of the difficulty in determining longitude, it was not known exactly where the Moluccas lay in relation to this point. Certainly, they were so far east of Malaya that even Portuguese cosmographers had begun to doubt Portugal's claim to them. Could it be that the richest islands of the East actually lay just beyond Portugal's domain?

If this were so, Magellan reasoned, then Spain had every right to exploit the Spice Islands. But she would have to find a new route there, since only at the risk of war could Spanish ships cross the Portuguese-controlled Indian Ocean. This was why he proposed to find the strait Faleiro spoke of. Once through this strait, a ship had only to sail northwest across the Pacific to reach the Moluccas.

In the fall of 1517, Magellan left his native Portugal, taking several experienced Portuguese pilots with him, to lay his plan before Spain's King Charles. The boyish monarch embraced Magellan's scheme with enthusiasm. By March, 1518, he had drawn up a formal agreement in which he appointed Magellan captain-general of the proposed expedition, promised him ships, made him governor of all lands he might discover, and gave him powers of life or death over all who sailed with him. The five ships Magellan was given were small and ancient, but, under his supervision, the business of patching, refitting, and provisioning them was soon under way, and he was confident that they could be made sufficiently seaworthy for the voyage.

It was a better beginning than Magellan had hoped for. But it was not long before King Manuel of Portugal learned of Magellan's scheme and attempted to sabotage it. His agent in this attempt was Sebastian Alvarez, the Portuguese consul in Seville. Alvarez's first move was to ask King Charles if it were true that Magellan and several other Portuguese seamen were being held in Spain against their will. Alvarez then hinted that, if Charles *had* detained Magellan, he had done a

Left: King Charles V of Spain, to whom Magellan turned when he left Portugal. The 17-year-old king was pleased to give the assistance for which Magellan asked and appointed him captain-general of the proposed expedition to the Spice Islands.

Above: painting by El Greco capturing the dignity and pride of Spaniards of rank of the period; a pride that could easily become contempt for foreigners, as Magellan found on his expedition with his captains.

wise thing, for a man who was disloyal to his own country might well be disloyal to another. Alvarez's sinister comments found their mark. King Charles began to treat Magellan with caution. He restricted the number of Portuguese seamen he could take with him and appointed several high-ranking Spanish officials to keep a watch on him during the voyage.

With Magellan, Alvarez used different tactics. He first urged him to save his honor by returning to Portugal, where he could count on King Manuel's forgiveness. Magellan replied that he preferred to keep faith with King Charles. Then Alvarez wished him good luck, and added that he would certainly need it. King Charles, he said, would doubtless suspect his loyalty and surround him with agents who would usurp his authority at the slightest pretext. Moreover, Alvarez said, the five ships Magellan proposed to sail in were so decrepit that he, Alvarez, would not risk a voyage to the Canaries in them.

Magellan was not so worried about his ships as worried about the possibility of his authority being usurped. Indeed, he became so afraid of mutiny during the voyage that he never allowed anyone to question his orders. In this way he precipitated a rebellion.

Despite Alvarez's machinations, the preparations for the journey continued. On September 20, 1519, the fleet left Sanlucar de Barrameda on the southern coast of Spain, and put out into the Atlantic. The five ships of the fleet were the *San Antonio,* the flagship *Trinidad,* the *Concepción,* the *Victoria,* and the *Santiago.* None of them was of more than 130 tons.

In the way of stores, Magellan had stowed on board essentials such as biscuits, cheese, wine, meat, beans, firewood, lanterns, lamp oil, tools, and utensils of all kinds, and also extras such as mustard, vinegar, almonds, garlic, raisins, medicines, fishing gear, and even musical instruments for the crew's amusement. Charts, instruments, and goods for barter he had in plenty, every item carefully listed. Nothing was lacking except confidence between Magellan and his captains.

All told, the fleet carried some 260 men. The majority of them were Spaniards. Next in number were sailors and pilots from Portugal, followed by a few men from other places. Among these were some Asians who had been brought to Portugal from the East and who might prove valuable as interpreters.

One of the crew members was an Italian named Antonio Pigafetta, who later wrote a vivid account of the voyage. Apparently Pigafetta

admired and respected Magellan from the outset. "The captain-general," he writes, "was a discreet and virtuous man… and did not commence his voyage without first making some good and wholesome ordinances." These "ordinances" were as follows. The flagship *Trinidad* was always to lead the way, while the other vessels were to keep within easy distance of it, maintaining a lookout for signals from the captain-general regarding making or shortening sail, changing course, and so forth. By night, every ship was to keep three watches, again keeping a sharp lookout for signals from the flagship which would be transmitted by means of flashing lanterns. Pigafetta explains why Magellan, who had never crossed the Atlantic, insisted on leading the way—despite the fact that some of the Spanish captains had more experience. "He did not entirely declare the voyage he was to make, lest men should not, from amazement and fear, be willing to accompany him on so long a voyage."

The Spanish captains must bitterly have resented not being taken into Magellan's confidence. As Pigafetta says, "The captains of the other ships did not love him." But Pigafetta seems not to have understood why. "Of this I know not the reason, except by cause of his being Portuguese, while they were Spaniards or Castilians."

The six-day trip to the Canaries, where the fleet took on more provisions, went smoothly enough. The first signs of trouble came during the ten-week crossing to South America. Instead of sailing directly southwest across the Atlantic, Magellan chose to follow the coast of Africa as far south as Sierra Leone before steering westward. This not only lengthened the distance to be covered, but also, by sheer bad luck, brought the fleet into exceptionally bad weather.

One day, the captain of the *San Antonio* hailed Magellan and asked why he was pursuing this strange course. Magellan, thinking he scented mutiny, replied sharply that no one must question his orders. A few days later, when he called all the captains to a meeting on board the *Trinidad*, the same man repeated his question. When Magellan haughtily refused to answer, the captain declared that he was not prepared to give unquestioning obedience to any and every order. This enraged Magellan, who at once arrested the captain and gave command of the *San Antonio* to another officer.

This incident seems to have had no immediate ill-effects, however, and the fleet sailed on. The ships were now passing through the waters of the southern Atlantic, and Pigafetta records with wonder the sight

of "sharks with terrible teeth, which eat people, dead or alive," and the electrical phenomenon known as St. Elmo's fire, which appeared as flames around the *Trinidad's* mainmast during tropical storms.

On December 13, the fleet reached the Bay of Rio de Janeiro. It was, of course, in Portugal's domain, but the Portuguese had not as yet established a colony there, so it was safe to rest at anchor in the harbor. After their long voyage, Magellan's men were allowed two weeks of ease, basking in the sun. They found the natives friendly and eager to engage in barter. Pigafetta reports that in exchange for a fishhook a seaman could obtain five or six fowls, while for a mirror he could obtain enough fish to feed 10 men.

On Christmas Day the fleet was still in the bay. The Southern Hemisphere's longest day of the year had come and gone. Moreover, Magellan knew that the farther south he traveled, the less daylight sailing hours he would have each day. He was anxious not to waste any more time, and on December 26 gave the order to sail on.

After two weeks, the five ships reached Cape St. Mary on the southeast coast of modern Uruguay. They rounded the cape in a storm and found themselves in the comparative calm of the Plate estuary. The next 23 days must have been bitterly disappointing for Magellan. Sailing west up the estuary, his fleet searched long and hard—but in vain—for a way through to the Pacific.

But surely the real strait could not be far away. Magellan decided to press on while the season was still young. The fleet continued southward, therefore, always on the watch for any other deep inlet that might prove to be the strait they were looking for. Late in February, a little south of latitude 40°S, they found the coast tending sharply to the west. Perhaps this was it. But no, they had merely entered the Gulf of San Matias, about a fourth of the way down the coast of present-day Argentina.

Doggedly the fleet continued to follow the coast southward for more than a month, the days always getting shorter, the land looking ever more barren, the temperature steadily falling. As March wore on, even the most optimistic of the men had to admit that winter was

Left: Freetown, Sierra Leone, West Africa, known for centuries as "the white man's grave" owing to the high rate of malaria and tuberculosis was discovered by the Portuguese in the 1460's. As in other places along the coast, they set up trading establishments there.

Above: picture of ships at sea in the 1500's, complete with monsters of the depths. At this period, when so much was unknown, the reality of monsters was as likely as any of the other wonders that were reported by sailors seeing lands not known before. A sea monster is not so different from a hippopotamus, if you happen to be unfamiliar with both.

Left: Magellan's route around the tip of South America, weaving through the strait which has been named for him.

147

Above: scarlet cock-of-the-rock, a brilliantly-colored bird found around the Strait of Magellan.

TIERRA DE PATAGÓNES

Above: the naked "giants" reported by Pigafetta in Patagonia. The Tehuelche tribe of this area gained a reputation as giants due to their large stature and physical vigor.

closing in—and still there was no sign of the strait. To continue the search meant facing ever-worsening weather. On March 31, near latitude 50° S, the five ships reached a sheltered harbor, Port San Julián. Reluctantly, Magellan decided to spend the winter there. Because the coast was barren, all the men would have to be put on short rations for the duration, but the captain-general saw no alternative but to wait until the warm weather returned.

The Spanish captains had long since given up hope of eventually reaching the Moluccas. On their side, the crewmen would gladly have exchanged the doubtful prospect of success for full rations and an immediate return home. But Magellan, already out of favor with the king of Portugal, dared not risk failing in his present mission and thereby earning the displeasure of the king of Spain as well. So, in spite of his men's objections to the plan, he began making preparations for the winter stay at Port San Julián. When it was learned that he would not change his mind, mutiny broke out. Pigafetta tells us that it was led by Juan de Cartagena, conductor of the fleet, and that it included many of the chief officers, who "plotted treason against the captain-general, in order to put him to death." Magellan learned of the mutiny in time, and put a swift and terrible end to it. "Cartagena... was banished with a priest... in that country called Patagonia" (in Argentina), and the other ringleaders of the conspiracy were executed and then quartered. Yet, by the standards of the day, Magellan was not unduly harsh. Many of the crew had been involved in the mutiny; Magellan punished only a few.

Most of the men were now willing to bow to Magellan's authority, and for nearly five months, during which some of the men died of the extreme cold, the expedition remained at Port San Julián. The only breaks in the monotony of their existence during this time were the occasional visits paid them by the natives of the surrounding region.

Above: Tierra del Fuego, an island at the tip of South America, separated from the mainland by the Magellan Strait. Magellan named the island to the south "land of fire," because of the custom of the Indians who lived there to build camp fires which could be seen burning everywhere.

Because of their giant stature, the Spaniards named these natives "Patagonians," meaning "big feet."

From late June onward, the nights began to get shorter, and gradually, as the noon sun climbed higher day by day, the cold abated a little. Magellan, anxious to be off, sent the *Santiago* southward to make an advance search for the strait he must find, and report back. Many days passed and the ship did not return. Finally, two exhausted men were sighted staggering along the shore toward the four waiting ships. A sudden squall had driven the *Santiago* aground near Rio de Santa Cruz, some 70 miles to the south. The vessel was beyond repair, and these two men had been sent overland to secure help for the stranded crew.

Rescuing the men of the *Santiago* took time. It was late August before the fleet left Port San Julián, and mid-October before they finally set sail from Rio de Santa Cruz. Just three days later they came to the Cabo Virgenes, where what seemed to be a strait opened out toward the west. This was, indeed, the waterway which Magellan had set out to find so many months before. By evil luck he had wasted a whole winter within 300 miles of it.

There was more ill fortune to follow. This strait, between the mainland and Tierra del Fuego, the large island just south of it, was like one of the great mountain-flanked fiords of Norway. It had many twists and turns, and often it divided into two channels, one running north, the other south. Supplies were running short, and Magellan could not waste the whole fleet's time exploring every channel. At one point, therefore, he decided to divide his fleet in two. The *Trinidad* and *Victoria* were to follow one channel, the *San Antonio* and *Concepcion* another. Some days later the *Concepcion* hurried after the *Trinidad* and the *Victoria* with the good news that the channel it had followed led almost certainly into the Pacific. But the *San Antonio* had disappeared. (She had, in fact, deserted, and was on her way back to Spain with vicious reports about Magellan's conduct, which, her crew alleged, had provoked a justifiable mutiny.)

On November 28, the three remaining vessels emerged from what was named the Strait of Magellan and entered the vast waters of the Pacific. As they did so, all three ships fired a salute and the captain-gen-

Right: this map from Pigafetta's *Relation* shows the Strait of Magellan as being an uninterrupted passage. This is far from the truth, as Magellan discovered. The strait follows a tortuous path, twisting, turning, and dividing around the numerous islands along its length.

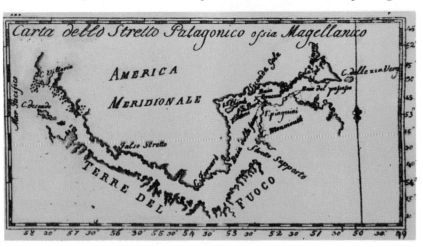

149

Right: an illustration from Pigafetta's *Relation*, showing the Islas de los Ladrones, "islands of thieves." This name was given to the Marianas by Magellan because, although not unfriendly, the inhabitants stole anything they could from the Spanish.

Below: painting on the ceiling of the church at Cebu in the Philippines, depicting Magellan planting a cross commemorating the first Christian baptism on the island.

eral wept for joy. Magellan had at long last found the southwest passage to the Orient. All that now remained was to voyage steadily northwestward until he reached the Moluccas. He little dreamed how immensely long that voyage would be.

For nearly two months, week followed week with never a sight of land. The remaining provisions dwindled to nothing, the last supplies of water became putrid, and the men were reduced to eating whatever they could find: ox-hides, grub-ridden biscuit, sawdust, and rats. (And even the rats were so few in number that they had to be auctioned off to the highest bidder.) The ravages of scurvy soon took their toll, and scores of men died.

At last, on January 24, 1521, the fleet sighted an island, which Magellan named St. Pablo. But it was barren and uninhabited, and the fleet was forced to sail on. A second island was sighted on February 3, but it, too, was barren. Then, after another agonizing month, the fleet reached some inhabited islands near Guam (about 1,700 miles northeast of the Moluccas). Here Magellan's ships anchored. The natives were friendly, but soon took to stealing whatever they could from the Spaniards. For this reason, Magellan named the islands the Ladrones, "islands of thieves." In retaliation for the loss of their possessions, the hungry sailors raided the native huts and helped themselves to as much food as they could find.

On March 9, with his crew partially restored to health, Magellan sailed west once more and reached the island of Samar in the Philippines. Here he gave the crew another two-weeks' rest before setting out to trade and preach Christianity in the nearby islands.

Early in April, Magellan reached the Philippine island of Cebu where, after doing some trading, he converted the local ruler to Christianity. Magellan then assured the ruler that if he had any enemies, he, Magellan, would crush them. The man claimed that he did have enemies on the nearby island of Mactan. Magellan, true to his word, set off with a party

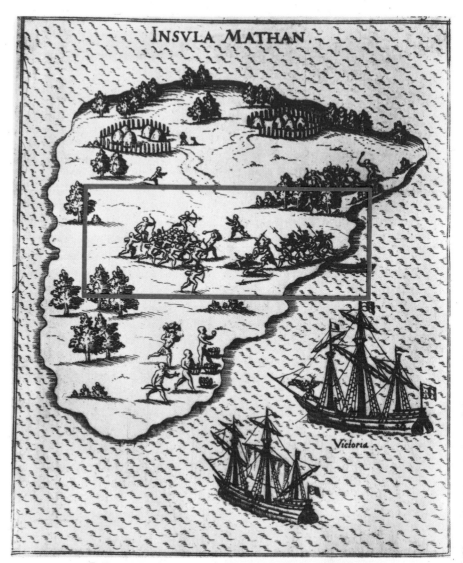

Right: the death of Magellan. This map shows Mactan, two of Magellan's ships, islanders offering gifts, and the fight in which Magellan was killed.

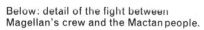
Below: detail of the fight between Magellan's crew and the Mactan people.

Right: old Portuguese fort at Malacca
on the Malay Peninsula. Captured by
Albuquerque in 1511, Malacca was for
many years a commercial base for the
Portuguese in southeast Asia.

Below: the route followed by Magellan's
men after he had been killed on Mactan.

of men to do battle with them. He was killed in the attempt, on April 27.

Magellan was then less than 1,000 miles northwest of the Moluccas.
Had he lived to sail 1,500 miles farther *west,* he would have reached
Malaya (where he had been some 12 years before) and become the first
man to circumnavigate the globe. As it was, that distinction would
belong to one of the Asians who accompanied the expedition as an
interpreter.

The failure of the Portuguese to crush the men of Mactan left them
wholly discredited in the eyes of the Philippine islanders. The recently
converted ruler of Cebu invited several of the fleet's chief officers ashore
and had them quietly slaughtered. The forlorn survivors of the expe
dition then set sail and, after taking on provisions at some nearby islands,

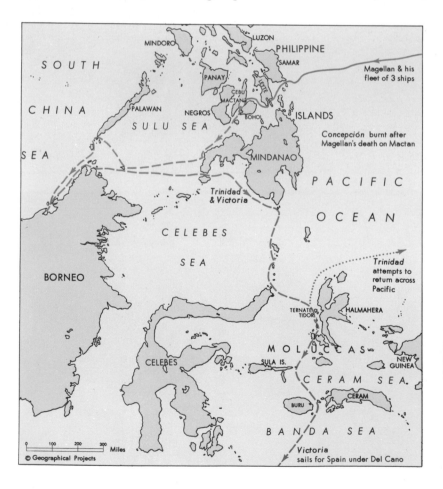

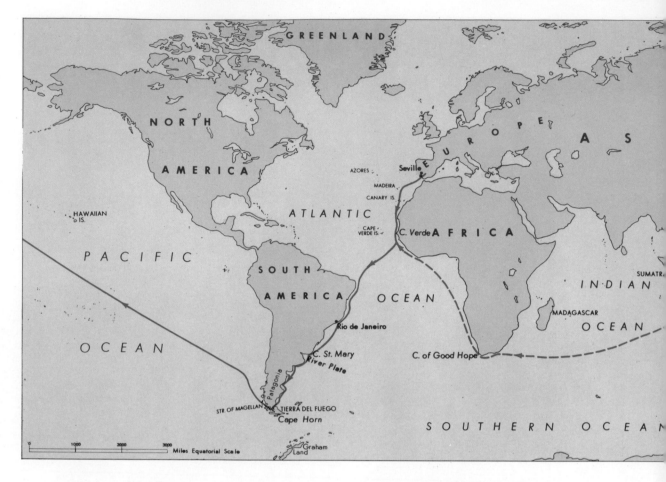

Above: Magellan's magnificent voyage circling the world. The broken line shows the return by the *Victoria* alone.

made for the Moluccas. But of the 260 men who had started on the voyage, only 115 now remained. There were simply not enough crew members to man three ships adequately. Thus it was decided to burn the *Concepción,* the least seaworthy of the three vessels.

Finally, in early November, 1521, the two remaining ships found their way to Ternate and Tidor, the rich Spice Islands to which Francisco Serrão (now dead) had begged Magellan to come. There the tired men of the *Trinidad* and the *Victoria* were received with splendid hospitality. They rested, bought food supplies, and took on heavy cargoes of spices.

When the time came to leave, however, the *Trinidad* was found to be hopelessly unseaworthy. The necessary repairs would take months, so it was agreed that the *Victoria* should sail home ahead of her. In January 1522, therefore, the *Victoria* set off for home alone. Her captain, risen to command as a result of the many deaths among the other officers, was Juan Sebastián del Cano, a former mutineer.

Del Cano might have retraced Magellan's outward voyage, but no one relished the prospect of another Pacific crossing, another passage through the Strait of Magellan, and possibly another winter in Patagonia. Wisely he chose instead to sail westward through the Malacca Strait, across the Indian Ocean, round the Cape of Good Hope, and then north to Spain. He would have to shun Portuguese ports and beware

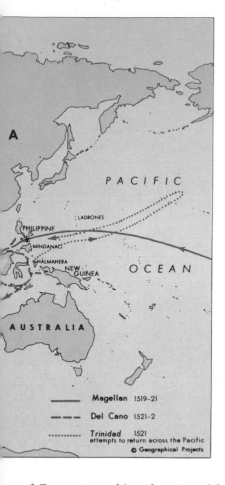

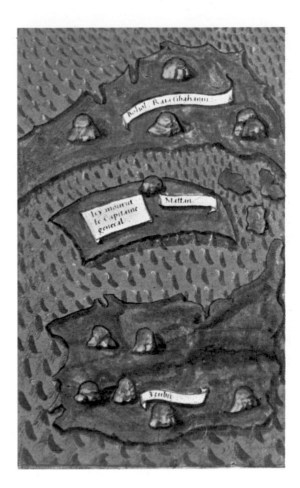

Above: Pigafetta's map of the Philippine islands of Mactan (where Magellan was killed), Bohol, and Cebu. As in most of his maps, Pigafetta shows south at the top.

of Portuguese ships, but the risks involved in sailing west seemed infinitely less great than those involved in sailing east.

Avoiding all well-worn sea paths, therefore, the *Victoria* made her way around the second half of the world. As she proceeded west, her food and water provisions steadily diminishing, one man after another died of hunger, fatigue, and scurvy.

But by mid-May, 1522, in a storm which smashed one of her masts, she had rounded the Cape of Good Hope, and by early July, she had reached the Cape Verde Islands. Here, even though he was in Portuguese territory, Del Cano was forced to make a stop. He succeeded in making the Portuguese authorities believe, however, that his ship was on its way back from the New World. The *Victoria*, he said, had been delayed by a storm, and stood in urgent need of food and water. The Portuguese, little suspecting the truth, gave the Spanish captain what he needed, and so made possible the completion of the voyage which King Manuel had tried so hard to sabotage.

On Saturday, September 6, 1522, the damaged *Victoria* at last reached the harbor of Sanlucar de Barrameda with her precious cargo of spices, and her exhausted, depleted crew. It closed a chapter. What men had been hoping for over a century had happened. They had reached the East by sailing west, and returned home again. The cost was tremendous but it had been proved it was possible.

Epilogue

Although he died before the completion of the first voyage round the world, the credit for this historic feat should really have gone to Magellan, for it was he who had made it possible. Indeed, in finding the western ocean route to the Orient, Magellan had achieved what Columbus had tried—and failed—to do. But it was to be many years before the world honored Magellan for the remarkable voyage which had cost him his life.

By the time the *Victoria* reached Spain in 1522, the mutinous officers of the *San Antonio* had long since returned home with their damaging reports about the captain-general. The *Victoria's* captain, Juan Sebastián del Cano, who had taken part in the attempted mutiny at Port San Julián, felt compelled to back their story. As a result, it was he, rather than Magellan, who was accorded recognition for the success of the voyage.

Meanwhile, the first circumnavigation of the globe had produced an interesting consequence for science. According to the crew of the *Victoria* and the ship's logbook, the date of her return was Saturday, September 6. But according to all land calendars it was Sunday, September 7. The reason for this apparent inconsistency, of course, was that the *Victoria* had crossed what we now call the International Date Line. But until this time it had not occurred to anyone that such a line would have to be established.

Strangely enough, the voyage produced no immediate results for navigation. In 1519, when the fleet had set out, Spain's American possessions had seemed of little value compared with the chance of a westward route to the Spice Islands. But by the time the *Victoria* returned, Cortes had completed the conquest of Mexico, and Mexican gold had begun to pour into Spain. This unexpected windfall naturally diminished the Spanish king's interest in spices or in the founding of an Eastern empire. (In any event, it was finally learned that the Moluccas did not lie in Spain's domain, but in Portugal's.) As a result, Magellan's western route to the Spice Islands was not used again for many years.

Yet despite this, the first round-the-world voyage stood out clearly as the culmination of an amazing period in exploration. In fact, it mark-

Right: the tower of Belém, built at the mouth of the river Tagus at Lisbon to act as a landmark and to protect shipping. The tower is incorporated in Lisbon's coat of arms.

157

Cappitaes Mores descubridores antes de auer Uisoreis e Gouernadores.

Annos de Christo.

1 — Bertolameu Dias _____ 1496. Descobrio o cabo de boaesperanca
2 — Vasco dagama descubridor da Sr da 1497. — Tornou ao Reyno
3 — P.º Alz Cabral _____ 1500 — Tornou ao Reyno
4 — Joaõ da Noua _____ 1501 — Tornou ao Reyno
5 — D.º Vasco dagama Almir.te da Jndia 1502 — Tornou ao Reyno
6 — Affonso de Albuquerque _____ Tornou ao Reyno
  — Francisco de Albuquerque _____ Perdeose
  — Ant.º de Saldanha e d.ª — Tornou ao Reyno
     erão cappitães mores — 1509
7 — Lopo Soares _____ 1504 — Tornou a o Reyno

Uisoreys e Gouernador

		annos / meses
D. Fran.de Alm.do g. S. Uisorey	1505	Morreo na cafraria gouernan — 4
Aff.º de Albuquerque Gou.or	1509	Morreo na Barra de Goa — 6
Lopo Soares Gouernador —	1515	Tornou a R.no gouernen — 3
Di. Lopez de Seq.ra Gou.or —	1518	tornou a R.no — 3
G. Fran. de Menezes Gou.or —	1521	Vai preso — 3
D. Vasco da Gama Uisorey	1524	Morreo em Cochim — 0 — 4
D. Henrique de Meñ. Gou.or	1525	Morreo em sonanor — 1
D.º Mascarenhas Gou.or	1526	Tornou ao Reyno —
Lopo Vaz de Sampayo Gou.or	1526	Vai preso — 3
Nuño da Cunha Gou.or	1528	Morreo no mar uindo preso — 9 — 10
Dom Garcia de Nor. Uisorey	1538	Morreo em Goa — 1
D.º Estevaõ da Gama Gou.or	1540	Veo ao Reyno — 2

ed the end of the beginning. In 1418, when Prince Henry the Navigator had set up his school near Sagres, European seamen had known only the coasts of Europe and the Mediterranean. Now, a little more than 100 years later, they had gained familiarity with the entire coast of Africa and almost all the southern coast of Asia, as well as much of Asia's east coast and many of its adjacent islands. They had roughly charted most of the Atlantic coast of North and South America, and even explored a few stretches of the two continents' Pacific coast.

In a single century, tremendous strides had been taken in discovering and exploring the world beyond Europe's shores. But that discovery and exploration had primarily been limited to the coastline of the world's great continents. In the New World, no Europeans except for Cortes and his soldiers had as yet penetrated far inland. In Asia, the activities of the Portuguese merchants, missionaries, and settlers were still confined to the areas within easy reach of fortified ports. Almost all of the deep interior of Africa was to remain a mystery to white men for more than three centuries to come. Australia, New Zealand, and Antarctica were as yet unknown.

Thus, when the voyage of the *Victoria* brought the first great phase

Above: Hieronymite Monastery of Jeronimos de Belém. The building was begun in 1500 by João de Castilho, as a monument to Portugal's great seamen. Many of the country's famous men are buried there. Parts of the building have been restored, but the central gateway is original.

Above: portrait of young Christopher Columbus from the Franciscan Monastery of La Rábida at Palos, where he lived and studied while he made preparations for his voyage. The canvas itself has been slashed.

of discovery and exploration to a close, the world still contained as much of the unknown as the known. But the daring exploits of men like Dias, Columbus, Da Gama, and Magellan had whetted men's appetite for exploration. And as more and more adventurers left their native lands to explore the unknown, it became clear that the "Great Age of Discovery" had only just begun.

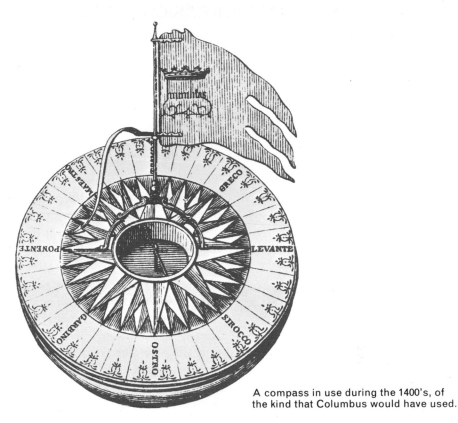

A compass in use during the 1400's, of the kind that Columbus would have used.

Appendix

In the preceeding pages we have traced the dramatic unfolding of the great age of discovery—the epoch of daring voyages that freed Europe from her enforced isolation and took her mariners to the far corners of the globe. Happily, this momentous period of exploration coincided with the growth of learning and literacy throughout Europe. Thus, one of the many things that distinguishes this age from earlier periods of discovery is that it is extraordinarily well-documented in contemporary accounts. Men who in earlier times might not even have been able to write their own names now possessed the ability, as well as the desire, to write vivid accounts of their own and other men's experiences.

The following pages provide a selection of documents written during and just after the period of exploration covered in this book. Ranging from the letters of kings to the journals of humble sailors, from confidential diaries to contemporary chronicles, they capture as nothing else can the unique spirit of this adventurous age.

To clarify the exact contributions of each of the explorers mentioned in the text, the appendix also includes a section of capsule biographies. An individual route map accompanies each biography, except in the case of explorers whose voyages have already been mapped in the text.

Glossary, index, and credit information complete the appendix. The glossary explains and amplifies the meaning of unusual or foreign words and phrases used in the text.

West Africa: First Impressions of the Portuguese

An African ivory carving of Portuguese soldiers. On the top is a little ship with a lookout in the round crow's nest.

The first contacts between the mariners of Portugal and the tribesmen of West Africa produced surprise and wonderment on both sides. The following passages from Cadamosto's account of his travels describe the initial reactions of the West Africans to the Portuguese.

"You should know that these people have no knowledge of any Christians except the Portuguese, against whom they have waged war for fourteen years, many of them having been taken prisoners, as I have already said, and sold into slavery. It is asserted that when for the first time they saw sails, that is, ships, on the sea (which neither they nor their forefathers had ever seen before), they believed that they were great sea-birds with white wings, which were flying, and had come from some strange place: when the sails were lowered for the landing, some of them, watching from far off, thought that the ships were fishes. Others again said that they were phantoms that went by night, at which they were greatly terrified. The reason for this belief was because these caravels within a short space of time appeared at many places, where attacks were delivered, especially at night, by their crews....

"These negroes, men and women, crowded to see me as though I were a marvel. It seemed to be a new experience to them to see Christians, whom they had not previously seen. They marvelled no less at my clothing than at my white skin. My clothes were after the Spanish fashion, a doublet of black damask, with a short cloak of grey wool over it. They examined the woolen cloth, which was new to them, and the doublet with much amazement: some touched my hands and limbs, and rubbed me with their spittle to discover whether my whiteness was dye or flesh. Finding that it was flesh they were astounded....

"These negroes marvelled greatly at many of our possessions, particularly at our cross-bows, and, above all, our mortars. Some came to the ship, and I had them shown the firing of a mortar, the noise of which frightened them exceedingly. I then told them that a mortar would slay more than a hundred men at one shot, at which they were astonished, saying that it was an invention of the devil's. The sound of one of our country pipes [bagpipes], which I had played by one of my sailors, also caused wonderment. Seeing that it was decked out with trappings and ribbons at the head, they concluded that it was a living animal that sang thus in different voices, and were much pleased with it. Perceiving that they were misled, I told them that it was an instrument, and placed it, deflated, in their hands. Whereupon, recognizing that it was made by hand, they said that it was a divine instrument, made by God with his own hands, for it sounded so sweetly with so many voices....

"They also marvelled much on seeing a candle burning in a candlestick, for here they do not know how to make any other light than that of a fire. To them the sight of the candle, never seen before, was beautiful and miraculous.... Having bought a little honeycomb, I showed them how to extract the honey from the wax, and... had some candles made and lighted. On seeing this, they showed much wonderment, exclaiming that we Christians had knowledge of everything."

The Voyages of Cadamosto, *trans. and ed. by G. R. Crone. Hakluyt Society, (London: 1937), pp. 20-21, 49, 50-51. Printed with the permission of Cambridge University Press.*

A slave gang in Zanzibar, with the Arab owner. Slavery had long been part of African life when the Portuguese came.

West Africa: Portuguese Trade Along the Coast

Very soon after the Portuguese began exploring the African coast, they established lucrative trading contacts there. This bill of lading, a receipt for goods received by a Portuguese captain in 1515 for trade near Arguim, gives us an idea of the kind of commodities they exchanged for slaves, gold dust, salt, and pepper.

Above: grain and spice merchants of the 1500's, when spices were luxuries available in Europe only to the wealthy.

Above right: harvesting cinnamon in the East Indies, from a book first published in 1575.

"Let those who see this bill of lading know that it is true that Goncalo Fernandez, master of the ship *Santa Catarina,* received from Estevam da Gama, captain of this castle of Arguj, these commodities, in order to go to pursue trade in the said caravel at Sete Moutas, whither he is now going....

   40 *allbernozes* [cloaks], ornamented with flock silk...
   28 coverlets of Alemtejo...
   44 hats of *bordate* [cotton]...
   4 hoods of Ipre cloth, green
   10 chamber pots
   10 shaving bowls
   2 tinned pots
   4 pairs of silvered stirrups
   6 pairs of silvered spurs
   2 pair of gilt spurs
   2 pairs of gilt headstalls
   2 pairs of silvered headstalls
   9 rods of pack-cloth
   50 combs, 50 looking-glasses, and 40 needles
   2 reams of paper
   32 alqueires of meal for the slaves
   19 bags of bisquit
   1 crossbow with its rack and 12 of its arrows
   1 handgun with its ramrod...
   2 spears
   1 lantern
   1 barrel of bread...
   1 chisel and 1 *gyva* [fetter]

"Because it is true that he received all these things... I gave him this bill of lading, made by me, Jacome Botelho, clerk of this castle, and signed by both. Done in this castle of Arguj, on 30 July 1515."

Portugal lost no time in establishing her rights to the coastline explored by her mariners. This order, issued by King Alfonso V to his captains in 1480, illustrates the fierce protectiveness with which Portugal was ready to defend her interests along the African coast of Guinea from any foreign interlopers.

"To all who may see this our letter, we make known that, in order to defend, guard, and preserve the trades of Gujnee... we, by this present letter, give the following power, authority, and special command to the captains who at any time may be sent... to the said Guineea: if they meet any caravels whatever, or any ships of any people whatsoever of Espanha [Spain], or belonging to any other persons who are, or may be, on their way out to the said Guineea or on their way back, or who are in it... that as soon as such persons shall have been seized, without any further order or course of law, all may be and shall be forthwith cast into the sea, so that they may then die a natural death, and they may not be carried to these kingdoms or to any other parts, because they are to suffer punishment for trying and desiring to do something strictly forbidden and prohibited. It will be a good lesson to those who may hear or learn of it, to beware of doing the like."

Europeans in West Africa, 1450–1560, Vol I, *trans. and ed. by John William Blake. Hakluyt Society (London: 1942), pp. 120-121, 245. Printed with the permission of Cambridge University Press.*

Columbus: From Triumph to Despair

In 1493, when Columbus returned home triumphant from his first voyage to "the Indies," he wrote a long and jubilant letter to King Ferdinand and Queen Isabella describing his discoveries. It is from this letter, written at the high-water mark of Columbus' career, that the following extract is taken.

"Knowing that it will afford you pleasure to learn that I have brought my undertaking to a successful termination, I have decided upon writing you this letter to acquaint you with all the events which have occurred in my voyage, and the discoveries which have resulted from it. Thirty-three days after my departure from Cadiz, I reached the Indian sea, where I discovered many islands, thickly peopled, of which I took possession without resistance in the name of our most illustrious Monarch, by public proclamation and with unfurled banners....As soon as we arrived at that, which as I have said was named Juana [Cuba], I proceeded along its coast a short distance westward, and found it to be so large and apparently without termination, that I could not suppose it to be an island, but the continental province of Cathay."

Right: Columbus, who placed enough faith in his calculations to sail out across the uncharted western sea to reach the fabulous wealth of the East.

Below left: Columbus and his men take their leave from the port of Palos.

Below right: Columbus returns to report to Ferdinand and Isabella.

Ten years later, Columbus wrote a very different letter to the king and queen of Spain. In 1500, as a result of administrative troubles in Hispaniola, he had been arrested and stripped of all his former honors and privileges. Now, in 1503, penniless and prematurely aged, he was struggling to complete a voyage which he had had to finance himself. In despair, he describes his plight and chides his sovereigns for their ingratitude.

"For seven years was I at your royal court, where everyone to whom the enterprise was mentioned treated it as ridiculous; but now there is not a man, down to the very tailors, who does not beg to be allowed to become a discoverer. There is reason to believe that they make the voyage only for plunder, and are permitted to do so to the great disparagement of my honor and the detriment of the undertaking itself.

"It is right to give God his due—and to receive that which belongs to oneself. This is a just sentiment and proceeds from just feelings. The lands in this part of the world, which are now under your Highnesses' sway, are richer and more extensive than those of any other Christian power, and yet, after that I had, by the Divine will, placed them under your high and royal sovereignty... I was arrested and thrown with my two brothers, loaded with irons, into a ship, stripped, and very ill-treated, without being allowed any appeal to justice who could believe that a poor foreigner would have risen against your Highnesses... without any motive or argument on his side...?

"I was twenty-eight years old when I came into your Highnesses' service, and now I have not a hair upon me that is not gray; my body is infirm, and all that was left to me, as well as to my brothers, has been taken away and sold....The honest devotedness I have always shown to your majesties' service, and the so unmerited outrage with which it has been repaid, will not allow my soul to keep silence, however much I may wish it: I implore your Highnesses to forgive my complaints. I am indeed in as ruined a condition as I have related; hitherto I have wept over others; may Heaven now have mercy upon me and may the earth weep for me."

Select Letters of Christopher Columbus, *trans. and ed. by R. H. Major. Hakluyt Society (London: 1847), pp. 1-3, 200-202. Printed with the permission of Cambridge University Press.*

Vespucci: Setting the Record Straight

Above: the opening illustration from Vespucci's letter reporting his voyage.

Below: Amerigo Vespucci, whose name was given to the New World.

AMERICUS VESPUTIUS

With the publication of Vespucci's accounts of his voyages, a popular misconception grew up to the effect that Vespucci, rather than Columbus, had been the first to discover South America. The following extract is taken from a book by Bishop Las Casas, a noted historian of the period, who attempted to correct this view and set the record straight for posterity.

"It is manifest that the Admiral Don Christobal Colon was the first by whom Divine Providence ordained that this our great continent should be discovered, and chose him for the instrument through whom all these hitherto unknown Indies should be shown to the world. He saw it on Wednesday, the 1st of August, one day after he discovered the island of Trinidad. He gave it the name of Isla Santa, believing that it was an island.... But all was mainland, as in due time appeared, and still more clearly now is it known that here there is an immense continent.... It is well here to consider the injury and injustice which that Americo Vespucci appears to have done to the Admiral, or that those have done who published his *Four Navigations,* in attributing the discovery of this continent to himself without mentioning anyone but himself....

"The first who went to discover after the Admiral was no other than Alonso de Hojeda... owing to his having got possession of the chart which the Admiral had sent home of the mainland he had discovered....It is a thing well known, and established by many witnesses, that Americo went with Alonso de Hojeda... [but] Americo's silence respecting the name of his captain, which was Hojeda, and his care to mention no one but himself... have led foreign writers to name our mainland AMERICA... as if Americo alone... had made the discovery before all others. It is manifest what injustice he did if he intentionally usurped what belonged to another, namely to the Admiral Don Christobal Colon, and with what good reason this discovery, and all its consequences, should belong to the Admiral.... As it belongs more to him, the said continent should be called Columba, after Colon, or Columbo, who discovered it, or else 'Sancta' or 'De Gracia,' the names he himself gave it, and not America after Americo."

The Letters of Amerigo Vespucci, *trans. and ed. by Clements R. Markham. Hakluyt Society (London: 1894), pp. 68-69, 71-72, 76. Printed with the permission of Cambridge University Press.*

India: The Goal Defined

Perhaps neither De Covilham's journey to India nor Dias' voyage round the Cape would ever have taken place had not King John II made the decision described in this passage by João de Barros.

"[Because] whenever India was spoken of reference was always made to a very powerful king called Preste João [Prester John] of the Indies, who was reputed to be a Christian, it seemed therefore to [King John] that it might be possible to enter India by way of his kingdom.... Taking into consideration Ptolemy's general map of Africa [and] the *Padrões* [commemorative pillars] on the coast which had been set up by his discoverers... it appeared to him that if his ships continued along the coast they had discovered, they could not fail to reach the land where the promontory Praso was, that is, the limit of the country.... All these facts... increased his ardor for the design of discovering India [and] he determined to send immediately in the year 1486 both ships by sea and men by land."

The Voyages of Cadamosto, *trans. and ed. by G. R. Crone. Hakluyt Society (London: 1937), pp. 127-128. Printed with the permission of Cambridge University Press.*

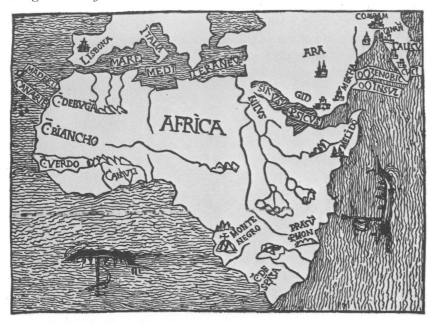

An Italian map of Africa, made in 1508, showing the Portuguese route to India.

India: The Goal Attained

Vasco da Gama's pioneer voyage to India in 1498 launched a new era in Portuguese history. The new-found ocean route to India placed the riches of the Orient within Portugal's grasp at last. Using this route, she could command a sizable slice of the spice trade and, in so doing, deal her old enemy, the Moslems, a severe economic blow. King Manuel I was delighted with these prospects, as shown by these extracts from a letter he wrote to King Ferdinand and Queen Isabella in 1499.

Above: the Portuguese merchants soon adapted to the style of life in India.

"Most high and excellent Prince and Princess....

Your Highnesses already know that we had ordered Vasco da Gama, a nobleman of our household, and his brother Paulo da Gama, with four vessels to make discoveries by sea, and that two years have now elapsed since their departure. And as the principal motive of this enterprise has been, with our predecessors, the service of God our Lord, and our own advantage, it pleased Him in His mercy to speed them on their route. From a message which has now been brought to this city by one of the captains, we learn that they did reach and discover India and other kingdoms and lordships bordering upon it; that they entered and navigated its sea, finding large cities, large edifices and rivers, and great populations, among whom is carried on all the trade in spices and precious stones, which are forwarded in ships (which these same explorers saw and met with in good numbers and of great size) to Mecca, and thence to Cairo, whence they are dispersed throughout the world. Of these [spices, etc.] they have brought a quantity, including cinnamon, cloves, ginger, nutmeg, and pepper, as well as other kinds, together with the boughs and leaves of the same; also many fine stones of all sorts, such as rubies....

"Moreover, we hope, with the help of God, that the great trade which now enriches the Moors of those parts, through whose hands it passes without the intervention of other persons or peoples, shall, in consequence of our regulations be diverted to the natives and ships of our own kingdom, so that henceforth all Christendom, in this part of Europe, shall be able, in large measure, to provide itself with these spices and precious stones. This, with the help of God, who in His mercy thus ordained it, will cause our designs and intentions to be pushed with more ardor [especially as respects] the war upon the Moors of the territories conquered by us in these parts which your Highnesses are... resolved upon, and in which we are equally zealous."

A week after reaching India, Da Gama obtained an audience with the king of Calicut. This extract from the journal of a sailor who accompanied Da Gama records what the captain said to the Indian monarch on this historic occasion.

Above right: Vasco da Gama at his audience with the ruler of Calicut.

"The king was in a small court, reclining upon a couch covered with a cloth of green velvet…. When the captain-major had entered, the king asked the captain what he wanted.

"And the captain told him he was the ambassador of a King of Portugal, who was Lord of many countries and the possessor of great wealth of every description… that for a period of sixty years his ancestors had annually sent out vessels to make discoveries in the direction of India… [That] there reigned a king now whose name was Dom Manuel, who had ordered him to build three vessels, of which he had been appointed captain-major, and who had ordered him not to return to Portugal until he should have discovered this king… on pain of having his head cut off. That two letters had been intrusted to him to be presented in case he succeeded in discovering him… and, finally, he had been instructed to say by word of mouth that he [the King of Portugal] desired to be his friend and brother."

The First Voyage of Vasco da Gama, *trans. and ed. by E. G. Ravenstein. Hakluyt Society (London: 1898), pp. 56-59, 113-114. Printed with the permission of Cambridge University Press.*

Brazil: An Accidental Discovery

Cabral's discovery of Brazil in 1500 was made by chance during his westward sweep through the Atlantic on his way to India. The following account of the discovery, written before the fleet left Brazil, is taken from a letter to King Manuel I by Pedro Vaz de Caminha, a man who sailed on board Cabral's flagship and who was official record-keeper on the voyage.

"Senhor:

Although the chief captain of this your fleet, and also the other captains, are writing to Your Highness the news of the finding of this your new land which was now found in this navigation, I shall not refrain from also giving my account of this to Your Highness, as best, I can, although I know less than all of the others how to relate and tell it well. Nevertheless, may Your Highness take my ignorance for good intention, and believe that I shall not set down here anything more than I saw and thought, either to beautify or to make it less attractive....

"And therefore, Senhor, I begin what I have to relate and say that the departure was on Monday, the 9th of March, and on Saturday, the 14th of the said month, between eight and nine o'clock, we found ourselves among the Canary Islands, nearest to Grand Canary, and there we remained all that day in a calm, in sight of them, at a distance of about three or four leagues. On Sunday, the 22nd of the said month, at ten o'clock, a little more or less, we came in sight of the Cape Verde Islands, that is to say, of the Island of Sam Nicolao, according to the assertion of Pero Escolar, the pilot....

"And so we followed our route over this sea until Tuesday of the octave of Easter, which was the 21st of April, when we came upon some signs of land, being then distant from the said island [Sam Nicolao], as the pilots said, some six hundred and sixty or six hundred and seventy leagues; these signs were a great quantity of long weeds, which mariners call *botelho,* and others as well which they also call *rabo de asno*. And on the following Wednesday, in the morning, we met with birds which they call *fura buchos*. On this day at the vesper hours we caught sight of land, that is, first of a large mountain, very high and round, and of other lower lands to the south of it, and of flat land, with great groves of trees. To this high mountain the captain [Cabral] gave the name of *Monte Pascoal* [Easter Mountain], and to the land, *Terra da Vera Cruz* [Land of the True Cross]."

Left: Cabral, swinging far west on his way to India, touched on Brazil and claimed it for the Portuguese.

Another letter written to King Manuel while the fleet was still on the Brazilian coast was by one of the expedition's astronomers, Master John. The letter provides an interesting (and rather amusing) discussion of the methods used for finding position and direction at sea, and, in addition, is one of the first documents in existence in which the constellation of the Southern Cross (which cannot be seen much north of the Equator) is described.

Below: woodcut of 1557 showing sailors taking observations using an astrolabe and the traditional cross-staff.

"Señor:

I, the bachelor Master John, physician and surgeon of Your Highness, kiss your hands. Señor: because Arias Correa as well as all the others have written to Your Highness at length concerning all that happened here, I shall write only regarding two points. Señor: yesterday, Monday, which was the 27th of April, we went on shore, I and the pilot of the chief captain and the pilot of Sancho de Tovar; and we took the height of the sun at midday; and we found 56 degrees, and the shadow was north. By this, according to the rules of the astrolabe, we judged that we were 17 degrees from the equinoctial and consequently had the height of the antarctic pole in 17 degrees, as is manifest in the sphere. And this is what concerns one point....

"In regard, Señor, to the other point. Your Highness will know that I have done whatever work I could concerning the stars, but not much, because of a very bad leg which I have, for a wound larger than the palm of my hand has developed from a scratch; and also because this ship is very small and very heavily laden, so that there is no room for anything. I inform Your Highness only how the stars are located, but in which degree each one is, I have not been able to learn; rather it seems impossible to me to take the height of any star on the sea, for I labor much at it, and, however little the ship rolls, one errs by four or five degrees, so that it cannot be done except on land.... Returning to the point, Señor... these stars, principally those of the cross, are large, almost as those of Ursa Major; and the star of the antarctic pole, or south, like that of the north, and very clear, and the star which is above the entire cross is very small...."

The Voyage of Pedro Alvares Cabral to Brazil and India, *trans. and ed. by William Brooks Greenlee. Hakluyt Society (London: 1938), pp. 5-7, 36-40. Printed with the permission of the Cambridge University Press.*

Venice: The End ot the Monopoly

Word of Cabral's immensely profitable trading mission to India in 1501 soon reached Venice. Portugal's new sea-route meant, of course, the end of Venice's monopoly over the spice trade in Europe. That this was immediately clear to the Venetians themselves is shown in this extract from the diary of a wealthy Venetian, Girulami Priuli.

"1501—September. On the 9th of this month letters came from Lisbon of the 1st August. And through letters from Genoa and Lyons and other parts, it is learned that the caravels which were expected loaded with spices are in Portugal.... It matters little now what the quantity of spices is; but the importance is the finding of the voyage and the trade, which each year will carry a large quantity of spices. This news, as has been said above, was considered very bad news for the city of Venice, and some very wise people are inclined to believe that this thing may be the beginning of the ruin of the Venetian state....

"Today, with this new voyage by the King of Portugal, all the spices which came [to Venice] by way of Cairo will be controlled in Portugal, because of the caravels which will go to India, to Calicut, and other places to take them.... And when the spices lessen to the Venetians, then will also lessen the profit and the money.... Truly the Venetian merchants are in a bad way, believing that the [Portuguese] voyages should make them very poor...."

The Voyage of Pedro Alvares Cabral to Brazil and India, trans. and ed. by William Brooks Greenlee. Hakluyt Society (London: 1938), pp. 135-137. Printed with the permisson of Cambridge University Press.

The South Sea: How Balboa First Heard of It

Above: Vasco Núñez de Balboa, the first European to gaze out over the Pacific.

Below: Venice in 1480, when she still controlled the spice trade with the East.

In 1510, Vasco Núñez de Balboa became governor of the new Spanish colony of Darien, on the eastern coast of the Isthmus of Panama. Three years later he led a hardy band of men across the isthmus and became the first European to gaze upon the vast Pacific Ocean. The following extract, taken from the works of the contemporary historian João de Barros, describes the circumstances under which Balboa first learned of the existence of the great "South Sea" beyond the mountains.

"About this time [1511] a circumstance happened which opened a new field for the Spaniards. Vasco Núñez de Balboa, a sensible, bold, and vigilant man, being at Darien with his men, paid a visit to Comagre, lord of a province which bore the same name.... Comagre's eldest son being desirous to oblige his guests, caused several pieces of gold, valuable both for their workmanship and fineness... to be brought, all which he gave to Vasco Núñez and Roderick Enriquez de Colmenares, knowing them to be the prime persons. They immediately set apart the fifth of the gold for the king, and distributed the rest among themselves. When they were dividing it, some quarrelled about the best and finest of those pieces. Comagre's eldest son, who was present, observing it, ran to the scales, and threw all the gold upon the ground, saying, they need not fall out about such a trifle; but if they were so fond of it... he would show them a province where they might have as much as their hearts could desire. And having understood that there was great plenty of iron in Spain, of which the swords were made, he said there was more gold in those parts than iron in Spain....

Vasco Núñez and his followers having heard these tidings, were so overjoyed, that they thought they could never make haste enough to discover those countries. They rested there some days, getting all the confirmation they could of the sea being beyond the mountains... and the immense wealth the youth had mentioned; and being wholly intent upon it, they made haste back to Darien, to send advice to admiral James Columbus, and to the king, of the wonderful discovery they had made...."

Voyages and Discoveries Made by the Portuguese and the Spaniards During the Fifteenth and Sixteenth Centuries *(London: 1789), pp. 464-465.*

Albuquerque – The Taking of Hormuz

Afonso d' Albuquerque, who became the second Portuguese Viceroy in India, is considered the virtual founder of Portugal's empire in the East. One of his most important achievements was the conquest of Hormuz, the Moslem port which guarded the entrance to the Persian Gulf. His first subjugation of this city in 1507 (he conquered it again eight years later) is described here by the contemporary historian João de Barros.

"When Albuquerque arrived there [at Hormuz], Ceyfadim, a youth of twelve years of age, reigned, and over him Coje Atar, a man subtle and courageous, who hearing what been done by Albuquerque, made preparations, laying an embargo on all the ships in the harbor, and hiring troops from the neighboring provinces, so that when Albuquerque came there were in the town thirty thousand fighting men... and in the harbor four hundred vessels, sixty of considerable bulk, with two thousand five hundred men.

"Albuquerque was not ignorant of the reception designed [for] him; but to show those people his resolution, he entered that port... and came to anchor between five of their greatest ships.... [The captain of one of these vessels] presently came on board Albuquerque's ship, and was received by him with civility and state. Albuquerque told him he had orders from Emanuel [King Manuel I] to take the king of Ormuz [Hormuz] into protection, and grant him leave to trade in those seas, provided he paid a reasonable tribute; but if he refused, his orders were to make war....

"The Moor delivered this message to the king and his governor Coje Atar, and presently... brought answer that the city of Ormuz used not to pay but to receive tribute. Night coming on, it appeared they prepared to fight, by the noise of warlike instruments, and shouts that were heard from the wall and ships.

"The morning discovered the walls, shore, and vessels, covered with armed men; the windows and tops of the houses filled with both sexes and all ages, as spectators of what should ensue. Albuquerque having held a council, and given necessary orders, began to play his cannon furiously, and was answered by the enemy. They taking advantage of the smoke, which hindered the fight, attacked the Portuguese ships with one hundred and thirty boats, well manned, which did some damage with showers of arrows, but received more, many being sunk, and the rest forced to retire by the Portuguese artillery.

The Arabs fought fiercely to protect their lucrative trade monopoly in India.

Yet they made a second attack, but were so received, that the sea was colored with blood.

"By this time Albuquerque had sunk two of the great ships, and had taken a third, though with great opposition, forcing the Moors to leap into the sea. The mean time the other captains had mastered other ships, and perceiving themselves victorious ran along the shore, and set fire to above thirty ships, which cutting their cables, were driven flaming upon the Persian coast, where they burnt others that lay aground....

"Coje Atar, considering the damage received, and what might ensue, called a council, where it was agreed to submit to what was demanded by Albuquerque. The articles were drawn, and sworn to by both parties; their substance was, that the king of Ormuz did submit himself to King Emmanuel, with the tribute of fifteen thousand xeraphins yearly... and should assign the Portuguese a place to build a fort."

Voyages and Discoveries Made by the Portuguese and the Spaniards During the Fifteenth and Sixteenth Centuries *(London: 1789), pp. 391-392.*

Magellan: Death at Mactan

Shortly after his arrival at the Philippine islands of Cebu, Magellan succeeded in converting the king to Christianity. As a mark of friendship, Magellan then undertook to do battle for the king with his enemies on the neighboring island of Mactan. The ensuing encounter between the Europeans and the Mactan islanders was a harrowing struggle in which Magellan himself ultimately lost his life. The episode is described in this passage from Pigafetta's account.

"We reached Mactan three hours before dawn. The captain did not wish us to fight then, but sent a message to the natives... to the effect that if they would obey the king of Spagnia, recognize the Christian king [of the island of Cebu] as their sovereign, and pay us our tribute, he would be their friend; but that if they wished otherwise, they should see how our lances wounded. They replied that if we had lances they had lances of bamboo and stakes hardened with fire. [They asked us] not to proceed to attack them at once, but to wait until morning.... They said that in order to induce us to go in search of them; for they had dug certain pitholes between the houses in order that we might fall into them.

"When morning came forty-nine of us leaped into the water up to our thighs, and walked through water for more than two crossbow flights before we could reach the shore. The boats could not approach nearer because of certain rock in the water. The other eleven men remained behind to guard the boats.

"When we reached land, those men had formed in three divisions to the number of more than one thousand five hundred persons. When they saw us, they charged down upon us with exceeding loud cries, two divisions on our flanks and the other on our front. When the captain saw that, he formed us into two divisions, and thus did we begin to fight.... When our muskets were discharged, the natives would never stand still, but leaped hither and thither, covering themselves with their shields. They shot so many arrows at us and hurled so many bamboo spears (some of them tipped with iron) at the captain-general, besides pointed stakes hardened with fire, stones, and mud, that we could scarcely defend ourselves....

"So many of them charged down upon us that they shot the captain through the right leg with a poisoned arrow. On that account, he ordered us to retire slowly, but the men took to flight, except six or eight of us who remained with the captain.... The mortars in the boats

Magellan works out his position as the *Victoria* sails into the unknown Pacific.

could not aid us as they were too far away. So we continued to retire for more than a good crossbow flight from the shore, always fighting up to our knees in the water.

"The natives continued to pursue us, and picking up the same spear four or six times, hurled it at us again and again. Recognizing the captain, so many turned upon him that they knocked his helmet off his head twice, but he always stood firmly like a good knight, together with some others. Thus did we fight for more than one hour, refusing to retire farther. An Indian hurled a bamboo spear into the captain's face, but the latter immediately killed him with his lance, which he left in the Indian's body. Then, trying to lay hand on sword, he could draw it out but halfway, because he had been wounded in the arm with a bamboo spear. When the natives saw that, they all hurled themselves upon him. One of them wounded him on the left leg with a large cutlass, which resembles a scimitar, only being larger. That caused the captain to fall face downward, when immediately they rushed upon him with iron and bamboo spears and with their cutlasses, until they killed our mirror, our light, our comfort, and our true guide. When they wounded him, he turned back many times to see whether we were all in the boats. Thereupon, beholding him dead, we, wounded, retreated as best we could to the boats, which were already pulling off. The Christian king would have aided us, but the captain charged him before we landed, not to leave his balanghai, but to stay to see how we fought....

"Had it not been for that unfortunate captain, not a single one of us would have been saved in the boats, for while he was fighting, the others retired to the boats. I hope... that the fame of so noble a captain will not become effaced in our times. Among the other virtues which he possessed, he was more constant than ever any one else in the greatest of adversity. He endured hunger better than all the others, and more accurately than any man in the world did he understand sea charts and navigation. And that this was the truth was seen openly, for no other had had so much natural talent nor the boldness to learn how to circumnavigate the world, as he had almost done."

Magellan's Voyage Around the World *by Antonio Pigafetta, trans. and ed. by James Alexander Robertson. (The Arthur H. Clark Company: Cleveland, 1906) Vol. I, pp. 171—177. Reprinted by permission of the publishers.*

The Explorers

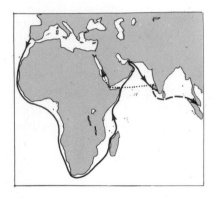

ALBUQUERQUE, AFONSO DE
1453—1515   Portugal
1507: Led a naval attack against
Hormuz, the Moslem stronghold at
the entrance to the Persian Gulf.
1509: Succeeded Francisco de
Almeida as Portuguese Viceroy
in India. During his six-year
rule, established Portuguese
supremacy in the East through a
series of brilliant conquests.
Set up Portuguese fortresses
from East Africa to Malaya.
1510: Captured Goa, one of the
richest trading ports in India.
1511: Led an expedition to
Malaya, where the Portuguese
conquered Malacca.
1511: Sent the first Portuguese
expedition to the Moluccas.
1515: Recaptured Hormuz, which had
attempted to throw off Portuguese
domination.

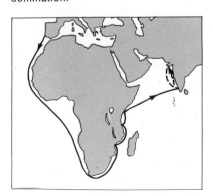

ALMEIDA, FRANCISCO DE
1450(?)—1519   Portugal
1505: Appointed Portugal's first
Viceroy in India by King Manuel
I. Set sail for the East in command
of a large and powerful fleet.
During his reign in India,
established many Portuguese
forts and carried on a
vigorous campaign against the
Moslems and their allies.
1509: Led the Portuguese in a
major naval battle against the
Moslems off the coast of Diu, India.
See map bottom of previous column.

BALBOA, VASCO NÚÑEZ DE
1475—1519   Spain
1500: Sailed west with Rodrigo
de Bastidas and settled in
Hispaniola.
1510: Stowed away on an expedition
to the Isthmus of Panama. Took
part in the founding of the new
colony of Darien and became its
governor.
1513: Led an expedition across
the isthmus in search of the
sea he had been told of. Became
the first European to gaze upon
the Pacific Ocean, which he took
formal possession of for Spain.

BALDAYA, ALFONSO GONÇALVES
dates unknown   Portugal
1434: Together with Gil Eannes,

was sent by Prince Henry to
travel beyond Cape Bojador.
Succeeded in reaching a point
some 200 miles beyond Bojador.
1435: On a second voyage,
traveled to Río de Oro.
See maps on pages 57, 73

CABOT, JOHN
1450—1498   Venice
1497: In the service of England,
sailed west in search of Asia.
Reached Cape Breton Island (off
the coast of Nova Scotia) and
Newfoundland, convinced he had
reached the shores of Asia.
1498: Explored the east and west
coasts of Greenland, sailed south
along the shores of Labrador to
Nova Scotia, and then continued
sailing south along the coast,
possibly even reaching Delaware
Bay, before returning home.
See maps on pages 93, 127

CABOT, SEBASTIAN
1474-1557   Venice
1494: Accompanied his father on
the expedition to Nova Scotia and
Newfoundland.
1509: Sailed as far as Hudson Bay
in search of a northwest passage.
1526: Visited Paraguay and the Río
de la Plata in South America.
See maps on pages 93, 127

CABRAL, GONÇALO
dates unknown   Portugal
1416: Was sent by Prince Henry
to find the reason for the
strong current between the
Canary Islands. It was the first
scientific expedition of this kind.
1431: Sailed westward in search
of islands which Prince Henry
believed existed in the area of
the Azores.
1432: Discovered St. Mary, an
island in the Azores.
1444: Discovered St. Michael,
another island in the Azores.
See maps on pages 57, 73

CABRAL, PEDRO ÁLVARES
1467(?)—1519(?)   Portugal

1500: Appointed by King Manuel I to command a large, well-armed, and heavily-laden fleet bound for India on Portugal's first major trading mission to the East. On the way, made a wide westward sweep through the Atlantic, and discovered Brazil. In India, was immensely successful in making commercial treaties with the rulers of Cochin and Cannanore, and returned home in 1501, his ships laden with valuable commodities from the Eastern markets.
See maps on pages 73, 76, 93

CADAMOSTO, ALVISE DA
1432(?)—1480   Venice
1455: Entered the service of Prince Henry and sailed on behalf of Portugal to the Madeiras the Canaries, and the African coast, where he touched in at Cape Blanc, Arguim, and the mouths of the Senegal and Gambia rivers.
1456: On a second voyage to the African coast, touched in at Cape Blanc, the Senegal River, and the Bissagos Islands (off present-day Portuguese Guinea).
See maps on pages 57, 93

CANO, JUAN SEBASTIÁN DEL
(?)—1526   Spain
1519: Sailed in Magellan's fleet as captain of the *Concepción*
1521: Became commander of the expedition after Magellan's death, and sailed the *Victoria* westward through the Indian and Atlantic oceans and up the coast of Africa to Spain.
1522: Back in Spain, received full credit for the first circumnavigation of the globe, though this achievement would have been impossible had not Magellan found the strait and crossed the Pacific.

CÃO, DIOGO
(?)—1486   Portugal
1482: Sailed down the coast of

Africa and discovered the mouth of the Congo River. Returned to Portugal after having pioneered about 850 miles of coastline.
1484 or 1485: On second voyage, landed at Cape Negro on coast of present-day Angola. Then proceeded as far south as Cape Cross, less than 200 miles from the Tropic of Capricorn.
See maps on pages 70, 73, 76

COLUMBUS, CHRISTOPHER
1451—1506   Genoa
1492: Sailed west in the service of Spain in search of the Indies. Discovered San Salvador, Cuba, and Hispaniola, although, to the end of his life, he believed he had reached the Orient.
1493: On his second voyage west discovered Dominica, Guadeloupe, and Mariagalante, and sighted the Virgin Islands. Set up a colony at Hispaniola.
1498: On his third voyage across the Atlantic, discovered Trinidad and sighted the coast of South America (which he mistook for another island). Traveled on to Hispaniola.
1500: Was arrested and divested of his position as Governor of Hispaniola.
1502: Final voyage west. Forbidden to revisit Hispaniola, he traveled down the coast of Central America.
See maps on pages 93, 130-131

CÓRDOBA, FRANCISCO FERNÁNDEZ DE
(?)—1518   Spain
1511: Went with Diego Velásquez to conquer and settle Cuba.
1517: Led an expedition which discovered and explored the coast of Yucatán. During this expedition, became the first Spaniard to find traces of the Mayan civilization.
See map bottom of previous column.

CORTE-REAL, GASPAR
1450(?)—1501   Portugal
1500: Sailed west to Greenland in the service of King Manuel I.
1501: Sailed again to Greenland and to Labrador and Newfoundland. Continued sailing south while his brother, Miguel, returned to Portugal. Never heard from again.
See maps on pages 93, 127

CORTE-REAL, MIGUEL
dates unknown   Portugal
1501: Sailed to Greenland in company with his brother.
1502: Sailed to Newfoundland in search of his brother, who had failed to return. Was never heard from again.

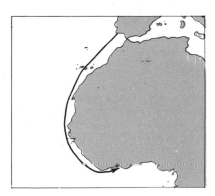

COSTA, SUEIRO DA
dates unknown   Portugal
1445: Sailed in the large fleet commanded by his son-in law, Lancarote, which traveled to Arguim and its adjacent islands

on a slave-raiding expedition.
1469: Sailed down the African
coast to Axum, on the shores
of modern-day Ghana.

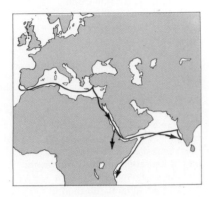

COVILHAM PEDRO DE
1450(?)—1545(?)   Portugal
1486: Sent by King John II to
find the land of Prester John by
traveling east to Cairo and
then journeying south overland.
Visited Aden, Cannanore, Calicut,
Goa, Hormuz, Madagascar, Cairo,
and Abyssinia (Ethiopia). The
reports he sent back to Portugal
provided positive proof that
a sea-route to India could be
found.

DA GAMA, VASCO
1469(?)—1524   Portugal
1497: Sent by King Manuel I to
pioneer the ocean route to India.
On the way, made a westward
sweep through the Atlantic which
took him within 600 miles of
South America. Stopped along
the African coast at St. Helena
Bay, Mossel Bay, Natal, Moçambique,
Mombasa, and Malindi. In Malindi
obtained a pilot to guide his
fleet across the Arabian Sea to
India, where he visited Calicut
and Anjediva.
1502: On a second voyage to the
East, he established several

colonies along Africa's east
coast, and, at Calicut, forced
the Hindu ruler to pay tribute
to Portugal.
See maps on pages 73, 76, 108

DIAS, BARTHOLOMEW
1450(?)—1500   Portugal
1481: Sailed to the Gold Coast.
1487—1488: Reached
farthest southern limit of the
African landmass. Rounded the
Cape of Good Hope, which he called
Cabo Tormentoso (Cape of Storms)
1497: Sailed with Vasco da Gama
as far as the Cape Verde Islands.
Then, on orders from King
Manuel, sailed to the Gold Coast.
1500: Sailed with Cabral to Brazil.
Died when his ship and five
others in the fleet went down in a
storm off the Cape of Good Hope.
See maps on pages 70, 73, 76

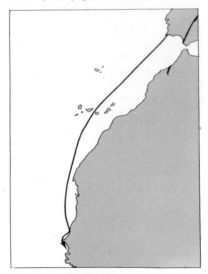

DIAS, DINIS
dates unknown   Portugal
1445: Set a new record by
voyaging some 500 miles beyond
Cape Blanc. Reached the most
westerly point of the African
landmass, which he named Cape

Verde.
1445: Took part in Lançarote's
large-scale expedition to Arguim
and its neighboring islands.

EANNES, GIL
dates unknown   Portugal
1433: Was sent by Prince Henry
to sail beyond Cape Bojador.
Returned to Portugal having
only traveled as far as the
Canary Islands. On a second
journey, succeeded in rounding
Cape Bojador, the first Portuguese
mariner to do so.
1434: Together with Alfonso
Gonçalves Baldaya, sailed some
200 miles beyond Cape Bojador.
See maps on pages 57, 73

ESCOLAR, PERO DE
dates unknown   Portugal
1469: Sailed as far as Elmina on
the coast of present-day Ghana.
1485: Sailed with Diogo Cão to
the mouth of the Congo River.
1497: Sailed with Vasco da Gama's
fleet as a pilot on the first
Portuguese voyage to India.
1500: Sailed as pilot with Cabral
to Brazil and India.

FAGUNDES, JOÃO ALVARES
dates unknown   Portugal
1520: Explored the coast of Newfoundland from Nova Scotia to
Placentia Bay.

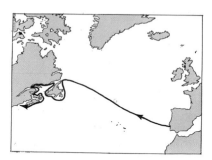

1521: Colonized the islands off the coast of Newfoundland.

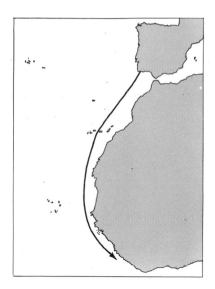

FERNANDES, ÁLVARO

dates unknown Portugal
1445: Sailing a caravel given him by his uncle, the explorer João Gonçalves Zarco, he rounded Cape Verde and continued traveling south until he reached the Cape of Masts, a point on the coast of present-day Senegal between Dakar and the Gambia River.
1446: Sailed down the African coast reaching a point on the coast of present-day Sierra Leone some 500 miles south of Cape Verde.

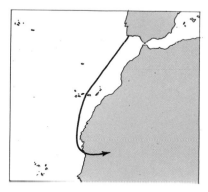

FERNANDES, JOÃO

dates unknown Portugal
1445: Accompanied Antão Gonçalves on his voyage to the Rio de Oro. Chose to remain behind when Gonçalves returned to Portugal, in order to study the land and its peoples. After living and traveling with the Berbers of the area for some months, returned to Portugal and reported to Prince Henry.

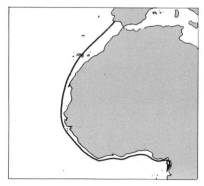

FERNANDO PÓO

dates unknown Portugal
1469: Discovered a large island in the Bight of Biafra, just south of present-day Nigeria, which he named Formosa, and which is now called Fernando Póo.

GOMES, DIOGO

1440—1482 Portugal
1458: Sailed down the coast of Africa to the mouth of the Rio

Grande. Then sailed up the Gambia River as far as Cantor and established trade relations with the local ruler.
1462: On a second voyage, he discovered, with Antonio da Noli, the Cape Verde Islands.
See maps on pages 70, 73

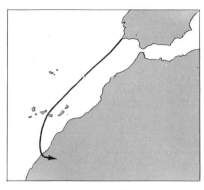

GONÇALVES, ANTÁO

dates unknown Portugal
1441: Sailed down the coast of Africa to the Río de Oro. On an inland raid, took a number of captives—the first ever taken by the Portuguese in Africa.
1443: Returned to Río de Oro.
1445: Again visited Río de Oro.

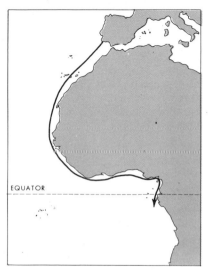

GONÇALVES, LOPO

dates unknown   Portugal
1469: Sailed down the African
coast, passing present-day Nigeria,
and possibly crossing the Equator.
See map bottom of previous column.

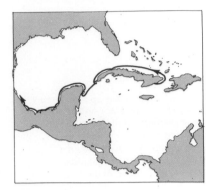

GRIJALVA, JUAN DE

1480(?)—1527   Spain
1518: Sent by Diego Velásquez,
the governor of Cuba, to explore
the Central American coast beyond
Yucatán. Reached the coast of
present-day Mexico, which he
named New Spain, and encountered
traces of the advanced culture of
the Aztecs.

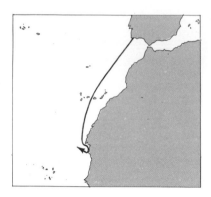

LANÇAROTE

dates unknown   Portugal
1445: Led a large-scale expedition to Arguim and its adjacent
islands for the purpose of
capturing natives for the
slave market.

MAGELLAN, FERDINAND

1480(?) — 1521   Portugal
1505: Sailed to India in the great
armada of Francisco de Almeida.
1509: Took part in the naval
battle against the Moors at Diu.
1509: Sailed in the first Portuguese expedition to Malaya.
1511: Took part in the first
Portuguese expedition to

the Moluccas.
1519: Set out, in the service of
Spain, to find a westward route
to India. After touching in at
Rio de Janeiro Bay, and stopping
at several other points along the
east coast of South America,
found the strait leading from
the Atlantic to the Pacific, and
sailed as far as the Philippines,
where he was killed in a battle
with the natives of Mactan.
See maps on pages 147, 152, 154

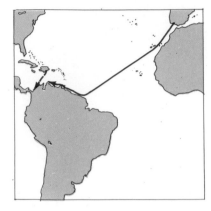

OJEDA, ALONSO DE

1465(?)—1515   Spain
1493: Sailed to the Caribbean with
Columbus, and took part in
setting up the colony at
Hispaniola.
1499: Explored, in company with
Amerigo Vespucci, the northern
coast of South America, from
present-day Surinam to the Gulf
of Venezuela.

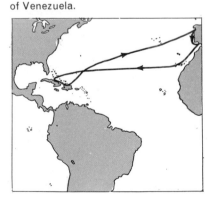

PINZÓN, MARTIN

1440(?)—1493   Spain
1492: Sailed as captain of the
Pinta on Columbus' first
voyage across the Atlantic
to the West Indies.
1493: Died, exhausted from his
labors, soon after completing
the difficult voyage back to
Spain.

PINZÓN, VINCENTE

1460(?)—1524(?)   Spain
1492: Sailed as captain of the
Niña, on Columbus' first voyage
across the Atlantic.
1499—1500 Sailed west across the
Atlantic to Cape St. Roque, on
the eastern bulge of South
America. From here, sailed
northwest along the coast to the
mouth of the Amazon, and then
to Costa Rica.
1508: Further explored the east
coast of South America in search
of a southwest passage to the
Indies.

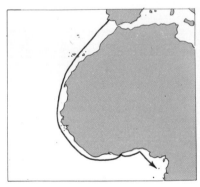

SANTAREM, JOÃO DE

dates unknown   Portugal
1469: Sailed about 100 miles
beyond Axum to Elmina, on the coast
of present-day Ghana.

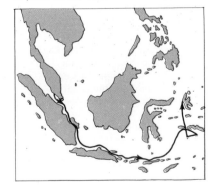

SERRÃO, FRANCISCO

dates unknown   Portugal

1509: Took part in the first Portuguese expedition to Malaya. During the battle at Malacca, his life was saved by Magellan.
1511: Took part in the voyage to the Moluccas. Although his ship was wrecked, he himself was rescued by the natives of Ternate. On this island, he chose to spend the remainder of his life. His constant urging of Magellan to sail to the Moluccas had much to do with Magellan's ultimate decision to find a western sea-route to the Indies.
See map bottom of previous column.

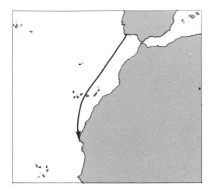

SINTRA, GONÇALO DE

dates unknown   Portugal

1441: Sailed with Antão Gonçalves to the Rio de Oro.
1444: Sailed down the coast of Africa to Cape Blanc, where he was killed during an attempted slave raid.

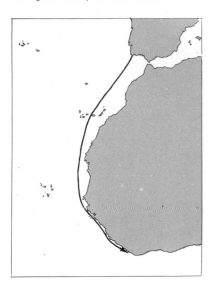

SINTRA, PEDRO DE

dates unknown   Portugal

1462: Sailed several hundred miles farther down the coast of West Africa than had anyone else so far, and reached the coast of present-day Liberia.

SOLÍS, JUAN DÍAZ DE

1470(?)—1516   Spain

1508: In company with Vincente Pinzón, explored portions of the South American coastline.
1515: Sailed again to South America and entered the Plate estuary, which he mistook for a southwest passage to the Pacific. Was killed by Indians some distance up the river.

TEIXEIRA, TRISTAN VAZ

dates unknown   Portugal

See Zarco, João Gonçalves.

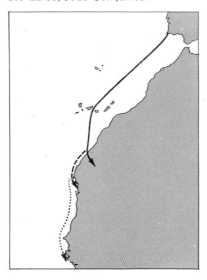

TRISTÃO, NUNO

dates unknown   Portugal

1441: Sailed some 250 miles beyond the Río de Oro to Cape Blanc.
1443: Explored the African coast from Cape Blanc to the island of Arguim.

1445: Sailed still farther south beyond Arguim to the point along the coast where the land ceases to be desert and becomes fertile.
1446: Sailed down the African coast some 200 miles beyond Cape Verde and died in a slave raid.

VELÁSQUEZ, DIEGO

1465(?)—1522   Spain

1493: Sailed to Hispaniola with Columbus.
1511: Headed the expedition which conquered Cuba and established the first Spanish colony there.
1514: Founded Santiago.
1515: Founded Havana.
1517: Sent Francisco de Cordoba to explore the coast of Yucatán.
1518 Sent Juan Grijalva to explore the Central American coast beyond Yucatán.

VESPUCCI, AMERIGO

1451—1512   Florence

1499: Sailed with Alonso de Ojeda, exploring north coast of South America from Cape St. Roque, Brazil, to Gulf of Venezuela.
1501: Sailed, in the service of Portugal, to the coast of South America, and, although his claims to having traveled as far south as latitude 50°S are not now believed, it is considered probable that he did travel as far south as latitude 32°S.
See maps on pages 93, 131

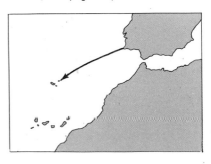

ZARCO, JOÃO GONÇALVES

dates unknown   Portugal

1418: Sailed with Tristan Vaz Teixeira to Porto Santo, one of the Madeira Island group.

Glossary

armada: A large force of armed vessels. The armada commanded by Francisco de Almeida in 1505 contained 22 ships and several thousand men. Often refers to the Invincible Armada sent by Philip II of Spain against England in 1588.

astrolabe: An instrument for measuring the altitude of heavenly bodies, from which latitude and time may be calculated. It usually consists of a wooden or metal disk, balanced from a ring and fitted with a sight rule which moves around a series of graduations for measuring altitude. Replaced by the sextant in the 1700's.

barca: A partly covered Portuguese ship of about 25 tons. It had one large mast with a square sail and a small mast which could be rigged if needed. Would carry a crew of 14 men.

barinel: Portuguese ship which had sails and oars. Larger and longer than a barca. It needed a large crew.

cartography: The art of mapmaking, a science dating back many centuries. The ancient Egyptians made maps as early as the 1300's B.C., showing boundaries of landed estates. Ptolemy was a famous ancient mapmaker in the 100's. He made a world map and 26 regional maps of Africa, Asia, and Europe, which formed part of his *Geography*.

caravel: First used in the mid-1400's by both the Spanish and Portuguese. They were ships of at least 50 tons, having three masts with lateen sails, and a castle aft. Later, as voyages became longer, the size was increased to 150-200 tons and another mast was added.

Catalan maps: Made by seamen from Catalonia, a region in northeast Spain. They were based on estimated bearings (from the seamen's observation of the heavens) and distances from ports and capes. The coastlines in between were surveyed to give a more detailed outline.

compass: A device used by mariners to determine the position and course of a vessel at sea. Consists of a magnetized needle free to rotate above a card, which is marked with points and degrees of direction. The card rests on a pivot so that it can move freely and always point to magnetic north. During the 1400's it was discovered that the compass needle did not point to true north but made an angle with it, and that the angle varied from place to place (magnetic variation).

corsair: A privately owned, armed vessel used for piracy and commissioned by an aggressive state or nation for war purposes.

Crusades: The holy wars waged against the Moslems by the Christians from western Europe between 1096 and 1270. Their aim was to regain possession of the Holy Land and to stop the spread of Islam.

dhow: A shallow vessel used by the Arabs on the east African, Arabian, and Indian coasts. It has a single mast with a lateen sail, the yard of which is extremely long.

doldrums: An area of calm or belt of light winds and sudden squalls found in certain sea areas around the Equator. One of the rainiest areas in the world. Mariners caught in the doldrums in the days of sail could be becalmed for days, or even weeks.

equator: geographical name for the line circling the earth midway between the north and south poles, which divides the Northern and Southern Hemispheres.

flagship: A vessel on which the flag officer commanding a fleet or squadron sails, and which carries his flag.

infidel: Generally, a heathen or unbeliever. Historically, used by Christians referring to Moslems and vice versa.

international date line: A voyager traveling eastward to the opposite side of the globe will be 12 hours in advance of the sun; one traveling westward, 12 hours behind the sun. To prevent confusion, the 180° meridian was chosen as a convenient point (the international date line) at which the date could be altered—forward if traveling west. backward if going east.

Islam: (In Arabic "submission to the will of God.") The religion practiced by Moslems, founded in the 600's by Mohammed. Born in Mecca in about A.D. 570, Mohammed believed that he was God's messenger sent to guide his people and call them to worship God (Allah). Historically, the word Islam is used to describe the geographical region covered by the Moslem empire (see *Moslems*).

lateen sail (or Latin sail): A triangular sail hung from a long tapered yard or pole suspended at an angle of 45° from near the top of the mast. Common in the Mediterranean and Indian ocean, lateen sails were first used by the Arabs on their dhows.

latitude: The position north or south of a point on the surface of the earth, relative to the equator. The equator has a latitude of 0°, the north pole 90° north, and the south pole

90° south.

league: A unit of distance varying between three and four miles.

longitude: A measure of east and west distance. Degrees of longitude are counted east and west of a line running through Greenwich, England, which most countries in the world have agreed is 0° longitude.

Marco Polo: (1254–1324): Venetian traveler who visited the East in the 1200's and was received by the Great Khan at Shangtu in 1275. He traveled extensively throughout the East in the Khan's employ. He was the first person to give details of a route across Asia, in which he described the kingdoms he had seen. In it he told of the wealth and great size of China. Christopher Columbus had a copy of Marco Polo's book and the notes he made in the margin show the great influence that it had on the admiral.

Meridian: Any single line of longitude i.e. any great semicircle along the earth's surface from the north pole to the south pole.

Moors: In ancient history the Berber peoples of northwest Africa who became Moslems and spoke the Arabic language. With the Arabs they conquered Spain in the 700's. Today the name refers to the Moslem people of northwest Africa who speak Arabic, or Moslems of Spanish, Jewish, or Turkish origin living in North Africa.

Moslems: People practicing Islam. They form the majority of the peoples of the Middle East, North Africa, Pakistan, Malaysia, and Indonesia. The first Moslems (the Arabs) began to establish an empire in the 600's and within a hundred years it spread from North Africa to eastern India. Moslems overcame the Persian Sassanian Empire and much of the Christian Byzantine Empire. They also threatened western Europe until defeated at the Battle of Tours in 732. Hundreds of different peoples were united into one brotherhood and Moslems established their culture in Iraq, Persia (now Iran), Palestine, North Africa, Spain, and Syria. It was through them that much of the knowledge of the ancient world reached Europe.

navigation: The science of finding a way from one point to another and of knowing at all times one's exact position. Navigate comes from the Latin words *navis*, ship, and *agere*, to direct. Before the invention in Europe of the mariners' compass in the 1100's or 1200's, sailors had either to stay within sight of land or to steer by the stars or planets. Modern methods of navigation date from the invention in 1735 of the chronometer, although it was not used widely until the end of the century.

The Orient (the East): The countries to the east and southeast of Europe and the Mediterranean, especially those of the Far East.

pilot: In navigation the name now refers to a person conducting a ship in or out of harbor. Formerly it was used to describe a steersman and the word "pilot" in this text would today mean the navigator. Amerigo Vespucci held the post of chief pilot of Spain from 1509–1512.

portolano: A Middle Age atlas containing charts (portolan charts) giving sailing directions, coastal and harbor outlines, and the location of ports.

Ptolemy: Ancient mathematician, astronomer, and geographer. He was born in Greece, but later lived in Alexandria, Egypt, where he practiced astronomy between A.D. 127 and 151. Ptolemy wrote many books and in his *Geography* the maps showed the landmass from Spain to China as larger than it is, and the ocean smaller than it is. This mistake had a profound effect on Columbus on his voyage of 1492, as his calculations of the distance he would have to travel to reach Cathay were largely based on Ptolemy's writings.

quadrant: A navigational and astronomical instrument for measuring altitudes. It is shaped like a quarter of a circle and marked with a scale on the curved edge. The sextant has largely replaced it.

St. Elmo's Fire: The glow of light which appears during a storm at the tip of a ship's mast or the spire of a church, caused by atmospheric electricity. The name derives from St. Erasmus, patron saint of Mediterranean sailors who looked upon St. Elmo's fire as a sign that their saint was looking after them.

scurvy (Scorbutus): A disease once common to sailors, caused by deficiency of vitamin C in the diet. The symptoms are pain in the muscles, weakness, spongy gums, from which the teeth eventually fall out, and bleeding in the tissues. Scurvy is easily cured by the inclusion of fresh fruit and vegetables in the diet.

Tropic of Cancer: Parallel of latitude about $23\frac{1}{2}°$ north of the equator. The northern limit of the Torrid zone.

Tropic of Capricorn: Parallel of latitude about $23\frac{1}{2}°$ south of the equator. The southern limit of the Torrid zone.

Index

Picture Credits

Listed below are the sources of all the illustrations in this book. To identify the source of a particular illustration, first find the relevant page on the diagram opposite. The number in black in the appropriate position on that page refers to the credit as listed below.

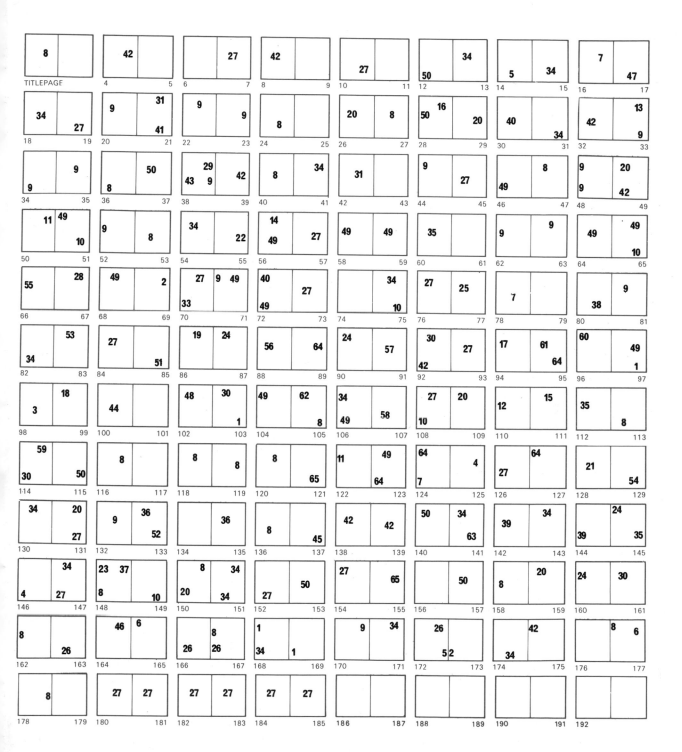